T0358394

Cambridge Elements ☰

Elements in Campaigns and Elections
edited by
R. Michael Alvarez
California Institute of Technology
Emily Beaulieu Bacchus
University of Kentucky
Charles Stewart III
Massachusetts Institute of Technology

STOREFRONT CAMPAIGNING

Joshua P. Darr
Syracuse University

Sean Whyard
Louisiana State University

Shaftesbury Road, Cambridge CB2 8EA, United Kingdom

One Liberty Plaza, 20th Floor, New York, NY 10006, USA

477 Williamstown Road, Port Melbourne, VIC 3207, Australia

314–321, 3rd Floor, Plot 3, Splendor Forum, Jasola District Centre, New Delhi – 110025, India

103 Penang Road, #05–06/07, Visioncrest Commercial, Singapore 238467

Cambridge University Press is part of Cambridge University Press & Assessment, a department of the University of Cambridge.

We share the University's mission to contribute to society through the pursuit of education, learning and research at the highest international levels of excellence.

www.cambridge.org
Information on this title: www.cambridge.org/9781009500708

DOI: 10.1017/9781009443357

© Joshua P. Darr and Sean Whyard 2024

This publication is in copyright. Subject to statutory exception and to the provisions of relevant collective licensing agreements, no reproduction of any part may take place without the written permission of Cambridge University Press & Assessment.

When citing this work, please include a reference to the DOI 10.1017/9781009443357

First published 2024

A catalogue record for this publication is available from the British Library

ISBN 978-1-009-50070-8 Hardback
ISBN 978-1-009-44333-3 Paperback
ISSN 2633-0970 (online)
ISSN 2633-0962 (print)

Additional resources for this publication at www.cambridge.org/9781009500708

Cambridge University Press & Assessment has no responsibility for the persistence or accuracy of URLs for external or third-party internet websites referred to in this publication and does not guarantee that any content on such websites is, or will remain, accurate or appropriate.

Storefront Campaigning

Elements in Campaigns and Elections

DOI: 10.1017/9781009443357
First published online: August 2024

Joshua P. Darr
Syracuse University

Sean Whyard
Louisiana State University

Author for correspondence: Joshua P. Darr, jpdarr@syr.edu

Abstract: Since Barack Obama's historic and unprecedented field operations in 2008 and 2012, campaigns have centralized their voter contact operations within field offices: storefronts rented in strategically chosen communities. That model was upended in 2020: Joe Biden won the election without any offices (due to COVID-19), while Donald Trump's campaign opened over 300. Using two decades of data on office locations and interviews with campaign staffers, the Element shows how the strategic placement and electoral impact of local field offices changed over the past twenty years, including differences in partisan strategy and effectiveness. This Element finds that offices are somewhat more effective for Democrats than Republicans, but Democratic field operations are declining while Republicans' are increasing. The Element concludes by assessing whether future campaigns will invest in offices again – or if the rebirth of storefront campaigning is over and the future of political campaigning is purely digital.

Keywords: elections, political participation, voter contact, campaign strategy, campaign organization

© Joshua P. Darr and Sean Whyard 2024

ISBNs: 9781009500708 (HB), 9781009443333 (PB), 9781009443357 (OC)
ISSNs: 2633-0970 (online), 2633-0962 (print)

Contents

1 Back to the Office

Driving into the Polk County Steak Fry on September 22, 2019, the innumerable yard signs for Democratic presidential contenders flipped past the car windows like a deck of cards being shuffled. Beto in black, Amy in green, Biden in white, Pete and Kamala in yellow, repeat. The sign wars between campaign workers started before sunrise, but the impressive aftermath greeted the 11,000 attendees entering Water Works Park in Des Moines, hoping to hear from the candidates – and while they were at it, buy a steak, baked beans, and potato salad to support the Polk County Democrats.

In addition to the heavy lunch, the county party supplied campaigns with an important resource that day: a space to organize next to the parking area. These spaces were roughly the same size but varied wildly in the ways campaigns put them to use. This physical space empowered campaigns to put their personality, resources, and enthusiasm on display, and allowed visitors to compare strategies and support side-by-side. Each campaign brought a bit of personality, intentionally or not.

The road to the Steak Fry bottlenecked just before attendees reached the parking area, and the Harris campaign guarded the pass with yellow shirts and purple signs. Tall black-and-white Beto signposts were held aloft behind them, his people obscured and resigned to the back half of the entrance point. The O'Rourke and Harris campaigns' allotted spaces were near the entrance, so they used that advantage and abandoned their tents in the early morning.

Once drivers fought through the bottleneck, the Biden campaign greeted them with the opposite of battlefield tactics. His space felt like a touch-a-truck event for children, with a pancake-making station, ice cream truck, and fire engine reflecting his endorsement by the Iowa Fire Fighters Union. A lone college-aged volunteer held up a Biden sign along the path.

The Buttigieg campaign purchased a $35 ticket for anyone who signed up through peteforamerica.com, and provided them with bright yellow shirts, rally signs with a one-day shelf life ("The Steaks Are Too High"), and choreographed chants. (The author in attendance, Darr, paid for his own steak.) Behind his bus, a large crowd milled about in hopes of seeing the candidate speak briefly.

Cory Booker supporters tossed footballs around, waiting for the attendees to come to them. Michael Bennet's volunteers played catch and cornhole on a hand-painted board next to a 12-foot-long prop gavel illustrating the *Des Moines Register*'s editorial observation that he was "pounding truth into the campaign" (*Des Moines Register* 2019).

Other campaigns clearly hoped to use the Steak Fry not only for the visibility but also to sign up supporters and make volunteers out of them. Warren's campaign formed several tight circles around their trained organizers, making sure that first-time volunteers knew what to do when the event began. Each received a "Liberty Green" helium balloon attached to their shirt so that Warren-friendly attendees could find them in the crowd. Everything ran like clockwork, connecting the volunteers' training to the candidate's speech pointing out the balloons, and culminating in her signature "selfie line" that stole away a good portion of the crowd once she was done speaking.

The Sanders campaign, on the other hand, did not show up except to place a prop. Their space featured a small tent and a door pulled from its hinges. A sign pinned to the door told interested attendees that Sanders organizers and volunteers were not there because, as the prop would suggest, they were out in Iowa neighborhoods knocking doors. Bernie's message was clear: the actual work of campaigning was knocking doors and playing into the pageantry of the Steak Fry was a distraction.

Harris and O'Rourke's teams used their geographic advantage by the entrance to make a first impression. Klobuchar and Buttigieg briefly spoke to attract curious attendees and energize their supporters for the walk into the event, though Pete could afford to give them shirts and tickets whether they actually supported him or not. Biden's campaign made sure his supporters were happy and well-fed, from the pancakes and ice cream outside to Joe's appearance flipping steaks on the grill inside. Warren took every chance to organize, train, and interact that it could, and the Sanders campaign made its point by leaving the space at the event unused, in favor of voter contact around the state.

Attendees could learn more about the candidates from walking around the parking lot than from listening to the repetitive and recycled stump speeches that rang out, twenty candidates deep, once the event began. That physical space allowed these campaigns to summarize, emphasize, and reinforce their philosophies and personalities by transforming a space to reflect their campaign's ethos and directing that energy outwards to find their voters.

1.1 Storefront Campaigning

On most days this sort of activity was happening in a campaign field office, not a field. Field offices are storefront locations that campaigns rent during the election season to serve as a base for their organizing staff to host trainings and events, volunteers making phone calls and heading out to knock doors, and interested passersby picking up literature or signing up for a shift. These local manifestations of national elections offer an entryway to political participation in a familiar and accessible location. Much of the work of elite-driven political participation – simply asking people to participate (Rosenstone and Hansen

1993) – starts in these temporary spaces in the strip malls and Main Streets of cities and towns across America.

In this Element, we examine the role of physical space in political campaign organizing in those field offices: a neighborhood-level presence in a community, set up as a storefront like any other small business. The retail politics that define competitive areas in presidential elections do not take place in a vacuum: they start with retail space. Canvassing conducted by motivated volunteers, the most powerful way to increase turnout (Gerber and Green 2000) and change voters' minds (Broockman and Kalla 2016), along with phone banking, are traditionally conducted in person and coordinated out of physical spaces that campaigns rent in strategic locations according to their perceptions of what is efficient and effective.

Using an original dataset on field office locations across the past three presidential elections and insights from conversations with former Democratic and Republican field organizers, we aim to discern the factors that influence campaigns' field office placement strategies; whether electoral outcomes are improved when a campaign sets up shop in a community; and how offices may have other benefits, such as staff morale, accessibility for harder-to-reach volunteers and voters, and improving participatory democracy. We argue that campaigns, their organizers, and their volunteers benefit from interacting and collaborating within the physical spaces of field offices.

We show that campaign offices help candidates in small but meaningful ways, delivering modest but quantifiable increases in candidate vote share in the areas where they open (Darr and Levendusky 2014). Field offices can increase candidate vote share, but their value differs across parties: Democrats benefit more in battleground states and populous areas, while Republicans' largely rural base of support in recent years provides challenges for maximizing the benefits of in-person organizing.

The 2016 and 2020 presidential elections were decided by razor-thin margins. Trump's 2016 victory rested on roughly 80,000 voters across Michigan, Wisconsin, and Pennsylvania, and his 2020 loss could have been a victory if 44,000 votes in Georgia, Arizona, and Wisconsin went his way (Swasey and Jin 2020). Small shifts in the most competitive states can and do prove decisive. Campaigns should look for every advantage possible where it matters the most, including the adoption of new communication technologies (Stromer-Galley 2014). The substantial organizational and financial resources poured into field organizing, even as digital voter contact becomes more widely adopted, show that campaigns think that in-person mobilization still matters.

American presidential campaigns bring people into the political process who had not previously participated and capture the attention of even the most infrequent voters. Where that contact is happening – on their television and computer screens or through personal conversations with members of their community at their doors and on the phones – is ultimately a strategic decision by the campaigns that may have profound implications for American politics (Stromer-Galley 2014). Directing national politics away from distant ideological divides and translating those issues into local terms can push back on polarization (Darr et al. 2018, 2021), and talking to people at their doors is the best way to increase political participation (Gerber and Green 2000).

1.2 The Ground Game

The "ground game" of localizing a national campaign stands in direct contrast to the "air wars" that defined advertising-driven campaigns in the late twentieth century (Darr and Levendusky 2014). Beginning with Barack Obama's 2008 campaign, which took their decided financial advantage over Republican nominee John McCain and implemented their candidate's community organizing ethos nationwide using nearly 1,000 field offices, the ground game reemerged in recent years as a major undertaking by campaigns from both parties.

After Donald Trump's surprise win in 2016, the stage was set for a revitalization of on-the-ground organizing in 2020. Some Democrats criticized Clinton's comparatively anemic turnout operations and over-investment in television during the campaign (Darr 2020; Masket 2020), and particularly her lack of travel to contested states like Wisconsin (Clinton 2017). The year 2019 and the early months of 2020 saw Democrats making efforts to return to their past dominance in the field. By the time Iowa's caucuses took place in February of 2020, four Democratic campaigns had opened twenty or more offices throughout the state: twenty-four for Warren, twenty-three for Buttigieg, twenty-four for Biden, and twenty-one for Sanders. These investments approached previous levels: Obama opened thirty-seven offices in the 2008 primaries, and in 2016, Sanders had twenty-three while Clinton opened twenty-six (Darr 2016).

Given that Democratic campaigns had opened more than 500 offices in each of the past three cycles, it seemed safe to predict that the eventual nominee would make a similar investment, and as in past cycles – where no Republican had opened more than 300 – once again dominate the "ground game" in the fall.

Things didn't work out that way. If you want to make the political gods laugh, tell them your plans from early 2020.

As in nearly all other aspects of life, the covid-19 pandemic in March 2020 dramatically changed the considerations of the presidential campaigns. Following his victory in South Carolina on February 29 and swift endorsement by his remaining opponents, it was clear Joe Biden would be the Democratic nominee.

Almost immediately, however, his general election campaign suspended any in-person voter contact activities: leadership was worried about public health and messaging concerns around knocking on voters' doors while the candidate was instructing people to socially distance, and they never lifted that ban through Election Day. The Biden campaign opened zero field offices in 2020. By contrast, Donald Trump and the Republican coordinated campaign (known as Trump Victory) charged ahead with over 300 offices in battleground states, establishing uncontested dominance with a field strategy deliberately built upon the model previously adopted primarily by Democrats. The Trump staffers we talked to, including Kevin Marino Cabrera, Florida Director of Trump Victory, were puzzled but pleased by the Democrats' decision:

> I think it was a strategic error on their part to cede the ground to Republicans. I think people were home, more than ever, and we found different ways to do it safely. Obviously you don't have to necessarily stand in front of the door, right, you can be a few feet back ... We found that people were home, more than ever, and that they were definitely looking to engage in conversation. (Cabrera, personal communication, July 18, 2022)

The 2020 experience increased the urgency of a simple yet critical question for campaign managers and scholars of American political behavior: does storefront campaigning work? Can field offices help campaigns move votes in their direction? Are they worth the substantial investments in rent, supplies, and salaries needed to open and sustain hundreds of offices nationwide?

The scholarship on field office placement and effects is mostly focused on the 2008, 2012, and 2016 elections, when Democratic candidates clearly held the edge in the field. After John McCain accepted public funding and its spending limits in 2008 while Barack Obama refused it, McCain was swamped in the field, on the airwaves, and at the polls. Figure 1 shows the progression of field offices over the past three presidential election cycles, where Democratic dominance is clear – until 2020, when it isn't there at all.

Mitt Romney leveled the financial playing field by refusing public funding in 2012 and raising comparable amounts of money to Obama, but did not come close to matching his efforts in organizing. Romney's 283 offices represented a substantial increase in Republican field offices but still represented less than half of Obama's total. According to analyses by Darr and Levendusky (2014), Romney's offices were more likely to be found in areas where Obama opened an office, and spread fairly evenly over swing and core counties (i.e. those that switched between elections and those where Republicans regularly receive over 50 percent of the vote). Romney's offices were less likely to be found in reliably

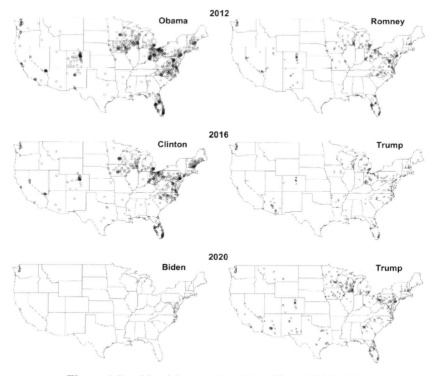

Figure 1 Presidential campaign field offices, 2012–2020

Democratic areas where Obama also had an office, and the reverse was true for Obama' offices. In short, Romney's 2012 campaign placed offices according to a similar strategy as Obama on a smaller scale.

The Trump campaign in 2016 represented a step back for Republican field organizing efforts, though Trump's campaign was ultimately successful in a lower-turnout environment. Trump only opened 165 offices, over 100 fewer than Romney. Unlike Romney, who was more likely to open an office in swing counties, Trump avoided contested areas in 2016 (Darr 2020). Trump's website did not even list office locations publicly until October. Field offices appeared to be an afterthought, as the campaign pursued a weak base activation strategy in some swing states (Darr 2020; Panagopoulos 2016).

Once the candidates were decided and the nation faced an unprecedented pandemic, it was clear that 2020 would play out differently. Shortly after the national lockdown was instituted in mid-March 2020, Democratic frontrunner Joe Biden indefinitely suspended all in-person campaign activities, as did the joint campaign operation of the RNC and Trump Campaign (hereafter Trump Victory). Around mid-May, word was sent to the Trump campaigners that all in-person campaign activities would start up again in June. Biden's campaign never opened a single field office.

The year 2020 represented a turning point for Republicans, with 319 Trump Victory offices – nearly double their number from 2016 – opening around the country. As we discuss in Section 2, Trump treated the Obama campaign as a "prototype" for victory and made the largest investment of any Republican campaign in the modern era (Kreiss 2016). Campaigns change course by adopting new tactics or shedding old ones following an election victory or defeat (Kreiss 2016). The next several elections will be crucial for determining whether voter contact goes digital or stays out in the field.

1.3 Offices Don't Vote

This recent history does not show that field offices are a "cheat code" for winning 270 electoral votes: Trump won with far fewer offices in 2016, then lost in 2020 to an opponent who opened none. While we offer evidence that storefront campaigning can be effective on the margins, we do not believe that offices alone make for a successful campaign or voter outreach strategy. The late-breaking, money-burning, ill-fated 2020 Democratic primary campaign of former New York Mayor Mike Bloomberg made that crystal clear.

After a fairly normal pre-caucuses process of opening offices and organizing, the nomination process began to crystallize after Joe Biden won the South Carolina primary on February 29. Buttigieg dropped out and endorsed Biden, as did Minnesota Senator Amy Klobuchar. Warren's campaign prospects were dim by that point after underwhelming performances in Iowa and New Hampshire, but she did not drop out. Biden staked his candidacy on South Carolina and only opened seven offices across all the Super Tuesday states. Sanders, on the other hand, was deeply invested in California, with more than twenty offices there alone, and opened many other offices in North Carolina, Texas, and Massachusetts.

None of these organizations could match the network of offices opened by latecomer billionaire Michael Bloomberg, former mayor of New York City, who declared his candidacy on November 19. After skipping all four early states, Bloomberg spent $500 million of his own money on his campaign, mostly concentrated on the Super Tuesday states. We found that Bloomberg's campaign opened eighty-six offices in those states, many more than his next closest competitor, Sanders (37). To build this organization quickly, Bloomberg paid his entry-level organizers the equivalent of a $72,000 annual salary, nearly double opposing campaigns' offer of around $42,000 (Ruiz 2020a), and promised (but later reneged on) job security through November regardless of whether Bloomberg won the nomination (Ruiz 2020b). T-shirts were free at his events, which were often catered with wine and beer and "goat cheese puffs . . . honey coated brie, fig jam and gourmet flatbreads" (Ruiz 2020a). The offices were no less swanky, featuring "terrarium walls" and custom murals costing thousands of dollars (Ruiz 2020a; Thomson-Deveaux 2020).

Bloomberg's campaign was mobilized so quickly, however, that they never built a volunteer base and instead relied upon $18-an-hour paid canvassers recruited through job listings on Indeed (Thomson-Deveaux 2020). This lack of enthusiasm, and abundance of paid staffers, was captured well by Amelia Thomson-Deveaux of *FiveThirtyEight*, who reported on the Bloomberg campaign in California: "Each time I set off in search of Bloomberg supporters at events across Los Angeles, his press staff warned me to make sure I wasn't talking to a campaign employee" (Thomson-Deveaux 2020). As a definitive illustration that money alone cannot buy organization, it was revealed in December 2019 that a Bloomberg contractors used prison labor to call voters (Wamsley 2019).

After Bloomberg won only one contest, American Samoa, he folded his campaign the next day. His over-the-top outreach operation paid off with roughly 6 percent of the available delegates on Super Tuesday.

Through Biden, Trump, and Bloomberg, 2020 showed clearly that offices alone do not make an organization. As we discuss the benefits and drawbacks of storefront campaigning throughout the Element, we should be clear that storefronts are not a silver bullet for campaigns. Bloomberg had all the offices, none of the organization, and flamed out spectacularly. Biden's general election campaign had none of the offices and narrowly won, while Trump tried to recreate Obama's community organizing-based model at a smaller scale and lost.

1.4 Preview of the Element

We use a unique and original dataset of presidential campaign field office locations from the 2012, 2016, and 2020 elections to discern patterns of office placement; conduct analyses on the influence of office placement on voting and turnout; examine patterns of political participation and campaign contact using large-N nationwide surveys; and test for possible moderating factors of field office influence, such as geography, ideology, and other campaign activities. These analyses continue and expand upon previous work on campaign activities, presenting a thorough examination of the past decade and more of competition in the field by both Republicans and Democrats.

Section 2 connects the literature on campaigns and participation to the theory and practice of field offices. Field experiments from Yale University showing that door-knocking is the most effective way to increase turnout encouraged campaigns to send volunteers to voters' doors (Gerber and Green 2000). More studies showed that personal and conversational voter contact was effective (Gerber et al. 2008; Issenberg 2012; Nickerson 2006), while others emphasized that targeting, effective scripts, and volunteer training are needed to reap the benefits (Bailey et al. 2016; Enos and Hersh 2015). We discuss how field offices empower campaigns to use these proven tactics most effectively while also bolstering staff morale and performance.

But where gets an office and where does not? In Section 3, we discuss the strategies behind office placement. Unfortunately for political scientists, campaigns do not randomly assign offices across all fifty states: they invest in strategically determined locations within the states they need to reach 270 electoral votes. This section builds on the placement analyses in Darr and Levendusky (2014) and Darr (2020), focusing on partisan, population-based, and competitive explanations for office placement at the national, state, and metropolitan levels. Using maps of strategically important metropolitan areas across recent cycles – Philadelphia, Milwaukee, Miami, and Las Vegas – we show how strategies vary across elections, even within the same cities. We expand upon previous work with analyses of the partisan breakdown of field office landlords and repeat use of spaces across cycles, as well as alternative explanations such as urban/rural breakdowns, local ideology (Tausanovitch and Warshaw 2014), and social capital (Chetty et al. 2022). These analyses and maps, combined with insights from our interviews with field staffers, provide the most thorough description yet of campaigns' geographic strategies for supporting volunteers and contacting voters.

Section 4 explores the kind of "forward progress" campaigns can expect from their ground game: small but potentially decisive given the incredibly close presidential elections of recent years. We update previous work on field office effects and add analyses that pool across elections (Darr and Levendusky 2014), quantifying whether field offices move votes and where Democratic and Republican offices might be more effective. We also examine moderating factors such as swing vs. core areas and urban vs. rural areas. Finally, using individual-level data from multiple waves of large-scale national surveys, we perform a multi-cycle "mechanism check" to show how field offices increase the prevalence of more personal methods such as door-knocking and phone calls.

In Section 5, we tackle the future of field. We discuss the unique circumstances of 2020, addressing what Biden's campaign did without field offices and how they used technological voter contact platforms and management systems to build community online. Having no general-election offices in 2020 was not the plan for Democrats, but the Biden campaign contacted millions of voters without them. However, we conclude that creating in-person space to meet and work is advantageous for campaigns. Organizers prefer working in an office; local volunteers are more effective (Sinclair et al. 2013); and localized appeals can make candidates more appealing to independents and across party lines (Munis and Burke 2023). As the pandemic's influence on everyday life dwindles, storefront campaigning should remain central to campaigns' voter outreach strategies.

1.5 Looking Ahead from 2020

We focus on the in-person aspect of offices, which can be distinguished from the broader tactic of person-to-person organizing in a digital era. The Trump campaign emphasized office-based organizing, but these innovations in campaign strategy inspired by Barack Obama's successful run and community organizing ethos do not *necessarily* require storefronts or even meeting in-person. Much of this recruitment and data-gathering could be coordinated through constant digital or phone communication between staffers and neighborhood team leaders, rather than meeting in a centralized location for these activities.

During the pandemic, the office-free model of organizing and voter contact – "distributed" campaigning – was put to the test by Democrats. While "local to local" may have been the ideal model, the covid-19 pandemic pushed Democrats to consider other ways to connect voters around identities and coalitions that did not require local appeals. Slack and Zoom replaced storefronts as places for volunteers and organizers to communicate with each other.

In September 2019, at that Polk County Steak Fry, there was no way to know how much the practice of campaign-driven voter contact would be changed by the covid-19 pandemic over the coming months and years. The 2020 election was an opportunity to reassess the role of field offices in the strategic arsenal of modern presidential campaigns. At an inflection point for the future of in-person organizing in presidential campaigns, we hope this Element can inform discussions about how presidential campaigns devote their increasing resources to reaching the voters they need for victory.

2 Why Storefronts?

From the perspective of a poorly paid, fresh out-of-college campaign organizer, working out of a shared physical space is preferable to solo online organizing for many reasons. This was the experience of one of the authors of this Element, Sean Whyard. Much like Elizabeth McKenna's experiences in 2012 informed *Groundbreakers* (McKenna and Han 2014), Sean's time in New Hampshire is useful for understanding exactly what the establishment of a local dedicated space means for those working on campaigns. In the paragraphs that follow, he describes some of those experiences.

Working as an organizer in the 2020 election was unlike any experience of my time in electoral politics. Prior to 2020, I would regularly see the opponent's organizers in a neighborhood, at a local coffee shop meeting prospective volunteers, or even at the same swing voter's door. 2020 did not work that way. In late spring and early summer, only one side was opening field offices, knocking on doors, and conducting a typical presidential ground effort: the Trump campaign.

My time during the 2020 election was spent working as a field organizer for the Republican National Committee in an often-overlooked but steadily competitive state: New Hampshire. With only four electoral college votes up for grabs, the state never receives the resources of other swing states, but in 2020, the Trump campaign poured substantial field resources into the Granite State. I started in New Hampshire in early February of 2020 and hit the ground running, recruiting volunteers and setting up my neighborhood teams.

At the onset of COVID, we noticed the Biden campaign indefinitely suspending all in-person campaign activities. The joint campaign operation of the RNC and Trump Campaign, Trump Victory, also stopped in-person campaigning shortly after the national lockdown in mid-March. The national slow-the-spread initiative sent our operation virtual within twenty-four hours. Instead of knocking on doors or meeting local volunteers at their homes, the field staff learned to organize virtually. In-person meetings moved to Zoom, and going to voters' doors was replaced with phone banking. It was clear, however, that senior staff knew a switch back to in-person contact was inevitable.

Once we returned in early summer, we were told our top priority was to scout retail space for field offices in our region of the state. The state's 'headquarters' office was established a few months earlier, but it was relayed to us that each region in the state needed at least one. My region, the southeastern corner of the state, ended up with two. As staffers, performing field organizing out of a physical space after months of virtual organizing was a welcome change that was far less stressful than the constant cold-calling frenzy of finding volunteers. Now, we could direct supporters to the office as a go-to regional location for campaign activities.

Shortly after I arrived in New Hampshire, I attended a full-day training session at the New Hampshire Republican State Committee headquarters in Concord. There, I was debriefed on our strategy for "the most extensive ground-game in the history of modern Presidential campaigns." That full-day training session included a crash course on how to organize: from recruiting prospective volunteers through cold-calling and attending local Republican committee meetings, to training volunteers on how to conduct voter contact, and then finally, creating "Neighborhood Teams."

Shortly after the training, I received a book from the deputy state director: *Groundbreakers: How Obama's 2.2 Million Volunteers Transformed Campaigning in America*, by two academics, Elizabeth McKenna and

Hahrie Han. I remember thinking it was unusual that a Republican campaign would base their organizing efforts off the successes of a Democratic president. Reading about how successful Obama's team was at activating volunteers to mobilize votes, however, made it clear quickly that this was just smart organizing.

I was instructed to read as much of the book as I could to better understand the 'Neighborhood Team Leader' (NTL) organizing model we were adopting. As an organizer for the campaign, my job in this model was to find an active and capable Republican activist with campaign experience. Once you could depend on a set number of voter contact hours per week from this person, they could recruit their own "team" of volunteers to work underneath them.

During my time as a field organizer, my life centered around the NTL model: recruiting volunteers, elevating volunteers to leadership roles, rinse, repeat. If my participation in the 2020 presidential election taught me something, it was that organizing, particularly this form of organizing, is arduous work. As strenuous as it might have been, working out of a field office proved immensely beneficial, as it provided a centralized hub for volunteer coordination and voter contact.

Throughout 2020, as Republicans rededicated themselves to offices, the pandemic pushed Democrats to rethink their field strategy and ask whether the basic activities of organizing – communicating with voters, giving callers scripts to use, collecting data on voters' preferences, and connecting them to their nearest polling place – could be done online, according to a senior Democratic official we spoke with who did not wish to be named:

There really wasn't anything, honestly, that you could do in a physical field office that we couldn't do digitally. The most important piece that we worried the most about recreating is that people come for the candidate but they come back for the relationships they make with their organizers, with fellow volunteers who live in the communities that they live in, who they may never have known. (senior Democrat, personal communication, September 1, 2020)

In this section, we will review evidence about the value of storefront campaigning. We start with an overview of political activism, organizing, and tactics, culminating in a discussion of the resurgence in field experimentation that pushed political practitioners back to personal methods of voter contact. Given that voters can be contacted digitally with modern technology (Stromer-Galley 2014), we discuss recent evidence showing that in-person interaction has intrinsic value that could help volunteers commit and stay engaged with a campaign. Interviews with Democratic and Republican organizers inform these discussions and suggest that increasing staff and volunteer morale may be the main appeal of opening an office.

2.1 Gathering with a Purpose

An active citizenry involved in voluntary associations is a hallmark of American life, whether through church and union membership, social groups, or political parties and campaigns (Putnam 2000; Skocpol et al. 2000; Tocqueville 2003). Social movements draw upon these skills, though not all social or political groups employ organizing as a main tactic (Ganz 2009; Skocpol et al. 2000). Despite the ideologically varied goals of social movements throughout American history, it is not uncommon for groups across the ideological spectrum – and politicians from both parties – to learn from each other's tactics, as presidential campaigns did with field organizing over the past twenty years.

Modern political community organizing owes much to Saul Alinsky, a political activist in Chicago during the Great Depression who organized Catholic churches and people from varying ethnic backgrounds to fight poverty in Chicago's Back of the Yards neighborhood. Alinsky formed neighborhood interest groups who were committed to clear, practical goals focused primarily on local issues (Stein 1986). Future presidential candidate Hillary Clinton wrote her senior thesis on Alinsky's organizing tactics and political ideology, and Barack Obama worked as a community organizer in Chicago in the 1980s under Alinsky-inspired organizing models (Schultz 2009).

Obama's 2008 presidential bid adopted a community organizing model that relied heavily on giving responsibility to trained volunteers (McKenna and Han 2014). Instead of building a temporary campaign on the fly with most voter contact falling on overworked and underpaid organizers or disinterested paid canvassers, Obama 2008 focused on building collective action through volunteer engagement at the neighborhood level (McKenna and Han 2014). Obama's campaign took Alinsky's motto to heart and directed organizers to encourage volunteers to act as change agents.

In this model, community organizing is assessed on its ability to successfully recruit, train, and retain volunteers (Miller 2010). The professional organizer serves as a catalyst to bring along other dedicated organizers in a volunteer capacity, who in turn take on the responsibilities of a leadership role: or, in Alinsky's words, "One should never do for others what they can do for themselves" (Miller 2010).

William F. Buckley, a prominent conservative activist in the mid-to-late twentieth century and the founder of *National Review*, admired Alinsky's disruptive and innovative organizing model. A new wave of conservative activists beginning in the 1960s embraced the lessons of Alinsky's writings, if not his politics, hoping to capitalize on the impact these tactics could have on mobilizing middle-class white voters. Buckley cautiously praised Alinsky and said he was "very close to being an organizational genius," and Republican leaders encouraged party activists to read Alinsky's book *Rules for Radicals* from the 1960s through the Tea Party movement in 2010 (Williamson 2012). Continuing this tradition, Brad Parscale, the campaign manager for Trump Victory until July 2020, became enamored with Obama's success in activating volunteers and began studying Hahrie Han and Elizabeth McKenna's 2012 book, *Groundbreakers: How Obama's 2.2 Million Volunteers Transformed Campaigning in America* (Berenson 2019; Cushman 2019).

There is a flip side to bestowing responsibility upon an army of unpaid volunteers, however: many of them hold political views that are much more extreme than the voters they are contacting on behalf of the campaign (Enos and Hersh 2015). From the perspective of campaign leadership, the relationship with volunteers is a "principal-agent problem": the staff may control the message, but they have far less control over the people delivering it directly to voters. The sort of person that willingly gives their time to a candidate is not likely to be a moderate who is on the fence about voting: rather, they are so committed to their politics that they will work for free to achieve their ends (Enos and Hersh 2015; Rosenstone and Hansen 1993; Zaller 1992). Without oversight and control, these opinionated volunteers might go off-script and harm their candidate. Offices provide the opportunity for door-knocking trainings and oversight of phone banking that could minimize the downsides of this principal-agent problem.

Obama learned from the mistakes of the past by emphasizing training. Former Vermont Governor Howard Dean's 2004 Democratic primary campaign activated extremely motivated volunteers, sending thousands of people to Iowa for a door-knocking blitz they referred to as "The Perfect Storm" (Stromer-Galley 2014). Many of these were first-time volunteers, and the campaign had more enthusiasm than organization. Canvassers were given a "Stormer kit" of an orange cap, blue stickers, and a penlight, and dispatched to Iowa neighborhoods (McRoberts 2004). As out-of-staters with little experience, these Stormers were poorly equipped for a campaign activity that is demonstrably more effective when conducted by locals (Sinclair et al. 2013). Obama's campaign tried to channel enthusiasm more effectively by bringing campaign volunteers to Chicago for "Camp Obama" sessions throughout the summer of 2007 (Schaper 2007).

Field offices not only implement the insights from data-driven campaigning, but also supply data back up the chain to inform estimates of individual voters' behavior. Enhanced data enables more precise targeting, which can increase turnout (Hersh 2015). Over the past two decades, these technological and strategic trends have converged to encourage campaigns to open field offices and deploy volunteers to not only act on the information they have, but also collect information directly from voters that factors back into the models.

Organizers provide the "boots on the ground" for this data collection at voter's door or on the phone, starting a more virtuous cycle that could empower better targeting and more effective interactions.

2.2 Field Research

The continued relevance of the ground game in presidential campaign politics was not necessarily guaranteed, given broader trends in the second half of the twentieth century. As technology advanced and the American campaign structure became top-heavy with consultants, media advisors, and fundraising, many believed the ground game would fall by the wayside (Rosenstone and Hansen 1993). Campaigns began to allocate most of their budget to fundraising and media as mass media continued to grow throughout the twentieth century.

In-person mobilization, traditionally the practice of local parties, was devalued as a necessary ingredient to win elections by the turn to television (Rosenstone and Hansen 1993) and was increasingly outsourced to PACs or community organizations. John Kerry's campaign utilized 527 organizations like his American Coming Together PAC to handle the voter contact duties. George W. Bush also outsourced his 2004 operations to churches, chambers of commerce, and other conservative-leaning civic organizations to get out the vote as part of his "72 hour plan" (McKenna and Han 2014).

The technological resources available to campaigns expanded exponentially in the early 2000s, and political science scholarship is at least partially responsible for its resurgence. Yale professors Alan Gerber and Donald Green conducted field experiments, which are high in both internal and external validity and based on actual records from voter files, to assess which techniques were most effective at increasing turnout (Gerber and Green 2000). Green and Gerber's book, *Get Out the Vote: How to Increase Voter Turnout,* served as a meta-analysis of field experiment literature and estimates that door-to-door canvassing produces at least a 7.1 percent increase in voter turnout, making in-person canvassing the "gold-standard mobilization tactic" (Green and Gerber 2019). The organizers we spoke to agreed with these findings: "There are so many ways to reach voters, but that still is the best way, a face-to-face conversation" (senior Democrat, personal communication, September 1, 2022).

Gerber and Green consistently found that messages with personal or social appeals are much better at getting people to vote than messages lacking that familiarity. Experimentation and optimization began to inform the scripts, modes of contact, and staffing decisions that campaigns made. Volunteer callers (Nickerson 2006), social pressure using mailers (Gerber et al. 2008), and lengthy personal conversations at the doors (Broockman and Kalla 2016) were most effective at turning out and persuading voters.

Practitioners adopted the lessons of this academic research and incorporated these mobilization strategies into their campaign operations (Issenberg 2012). Obama's 2008 campaign relied on experimental findings when crafting phone and canvassing scripts for use in tandem with reliable data modeling voters' preferences and propensity to turn out. Reliable and practical data became readily accessible in the early 2000s, but Obama's 2012 re-election campaign was the first to combine data from various streams (online sign-ups, donations, conversations, consumer data, etc.) into a single database that could be used for targeting, messaging, and mobilization (Baldwin-Phillippi 2016).

Implementing the strategies suggested by data operations still required old-fashioned effort from volunteers and organizers in the areas that mattered most, and Obama's team opened over 700 offices to make that happen. These techno-logical and strategic trends coalesced over the past two decades to encourage campaigns to open field offices and deploy volunteers to not only act on the information they have, but also acquire information directly from voters that feeds back into and improves the data they use.

2.3 A Place to Meet

Much of the research on voter contact came from the era of party-driven politics, where candidates were indistinguishable from state and local mani-festations of their party (Eldersveld and Walton 1982; Ranney 1956). Over time, television became the major expenditure in campaigns (Rosenstone and Hansen 1993), weakening the need for party support and heightening the focus on the candidate themselves. As campaigns centered more on the candidate, in-person mobilization was usually outsourced to organized labor or non-profit fundraising organizations (see Barone and Cohen 2006; Nielsen 2012). When extensive local organizing reemerged inside Obama's 2008 campaign, a new strain of campaign literature began to emerge examining the impact of these offices (Darr 2020; Darr and Levendusky 2014; Masket 2009; Masket et al. 2016).

Even in a world of billion-dollar-plus campaigns, leadership faces constraints on how to strategically allocate resources (Campbell 2008). At the turn of the twenty-first century, beginning with Bush's 72-hour plan and Kerry's help from a 527 organization, campaigns began to prioritize in-person connections and incorporate the ground game more than cycles prior (McKenna and Han 2014). A dedicated office space gives organizers a place to work and meet, distribute canvassing literature and walk packets, and help interested passersby navigate the voting system and find ways to volunteer (Darr and Levendusky 2014; Masket et al. 2016; Nickerson 2007; Nickerson and Rogers 2010).

The fundamental human need to connect with other people is an underlying mechanism for engaging in costly behaviors in a social environment (Leary and Baumeister 1995; McClelland 1985), which is directly relevant to campaigns trying to recruit and retain labor. When people gather collectively, their reported feelings of self-expansion and group identity fusion intensify (Besta et al. 2018; Reese and Whitehouse 2021; Swann et al. 2012; Whitehouse and Lanman 2014). Within a multi-day mass gathering event, for example, people's self-reported feelings of connectedness between themselves and others increased (Yaden et al. 2017; Yudkin et al. 2022). When in the presence of others, people have been shown to afford more importance to binding, rather than individual-ized, moral values (Yudkin et al. 2021), which is precisely the mindset cam-paigns want their volunteers to adopt.

Social gatherings are an effective voter mobilization tactic for campaigns, similar in cost-effectiveness to that of door-to-door canvassing (Addonizio et al. 2007). Most voting blocs, including young people, are more likely to engage in social political behavior when socializing with peers and attending GOTV festivals (Ohme et al. 2020). By incorporating more personal and interactive activities, and participating in socializing acts, the collective action dilemma is weakened, and people are more willing to engage in costly behavior like voting or other political behaviors (Addonizio et al. 2007; Ohme et al. 2020).

Evidence from businesses also shows why field offices might be particularly valuable for campaigns, particularly in the wake of the covid-19 pandemic. Using evidence from the call center of a Fortune 500 company, researchers found that workers were 12 percent less likely to answer calls when working remotely. In-person workers moving remotely during covid-19 accounted for about one-third of this productivity gap, with the remaining two-thirds due to remote work attracting lower-quality employees (Emanuel and Harrington 2023). Workers also received fewer investments in their skills and made lower-quality calls, particularly for new hires (Emanuel and Harrington 2023) – which, in the case of campaigns, should represent many volunteers.

These researchers also found that working in the same building led to more online feedback from their office mates for software engineers, helping them to grow, develop, and improve their work (Emanuel et al. 2023). These findings are particularly true among women, who give and receive more mentorship when sitting closer to their coworkers. The authors also find that productivity suffers when workers are seated next to others, suggesting some possible downsides of social proximity for productivity.

This evidence from the great experiment in remote work brought on by covid-19 shows that campaigns who are interested in mentoring staffers for future work within the party, giving feedback to improve volunteers' performance in voter contact, and generally ensuring higher quality interactions, should continue to place workers and volunteers in close proximity. While higher numbers of calls and texts can be sent using digital tools, these activities can be expected to attract lower-quality workers and present fewer opportunities for mentorship, training, and engagement (Stromer-Galley 2014). Given the potential of voter contact to alienate voters in some circumstances (Bailey et al. 2016), it is imperative that campaigns make quality contacts efficiently and effectively.

2.4 The View from the Storefront

For additional perspective on the campaign side, we interviewed four staffers at various levels that worked for Republicans or Democrats: Kevin Cabrera, the Trump Victory State Director in Florida, worked as a Capitol Hill staffer and served as an elected official for a zoning board in Miami-Dade County. Peter O'Neill worked as an organizer for several local Connecticut races before joining Trump Victory as a regional field director in New Hampshire; a senior DNC staffer with extensive experience organizing in multiple cycles, who did not wish to be named; and a college student taking time off to work in an Iowa Julian Castro field office in 2019 who also did not wish to be named. Our interview protocols are included in Online Appendix A2.4.[1]

Offices can help campaigns achieve other goals besides explicitly moving votes. Even national campaigns are constrained to selected local areas of focus by the primary process and the electoral college. Campaign workers are often far from home and living in supporter housing or cheap apartments but intrinsically motivated by the work: the Castro organizer felt the work was already worth it because of its civic contributions:

> I would be proud of my work as an organizer for sure. If you talk to just one person and that person registers to vote or actually does vote, then it makes it worth it. I've already registered people to vote, in a lot of ways it feels like it already paid off. (Castro organizer, September 18, 2019)

Cabrera described how offices could help reinforce these social and psychological benefits: "You know offices, if anything, they serve as a place for

---

[1] Campaign workers are difficult to locate during or after an election, and often reticent to discuss campaign strategy. While in Iowa, the author (Darr) tried to contact field staff directly, but was denied permission by campaign media relations staff. As such, our sample of conversations is fairly small and we cannot make truly generalizable inferences. We hope these interviews help paint a fuller picture of the value of offices that can complement our quantitative findings in Sections 3 and 4.

volunteers to go and to meet with other people and to make them feel confident that they're not the only ones" (Cabrera, personal communication, July 18, 2022). State-specific political culture and expectations may also influence field strategy from campaigns. In New Hampshire, for instance, decades of serving as the "first in the nation" primary has developed a strong tradition of retail politics in the space. O'Neill described how this built-in expectation influenced their strategy in 2020:

> Specifically in the state of New Hampshire, where retail politics is what makes or breaks a primary win, you can't not have a field office in New Hampshire. You could get away with that in other states – not in New Hampshire. I don't think that would be a wise decision for anybody who decided to run for president. (O'Neill, personal communication, August 2, 2022)

Campaigns' ultimate objective is to earn enough votes to win, and keeping supporters and staffers satisfied should help achieve that goal. This means not only a supportive work environment for staffers, but also forming the kind of environment and community that makes (unpaid) volunteers want to keep coming back while drawing in new people from the surrounding area. Calling voters and knocking doors is not always pleasant: in practice, outreach often means hang-ups and door slams. As the sites of this face-to-face interaction and collective action, offices may therefore serve campaigns as sources of morale for volunteers, activists, and paid organizers alike to find purpose and renew their energy during the many hours of work leading up to election day. A common meeting place to connect and commiserate with volunteers gives staffers and supporters somewhere to recharge and reconnect.

> (The offices) weren't just for political purposes but they helped build community. We had beautiful stories where folks would do karaoke in some of our offices, they would go watch UFC fights and different, you know, whether it be a baseball game, the World Series, whatever it may be, they use those offices, not just for political purposes, but for the sense of building community. (Cabrera, personal communication, July 18, 2022)

Volunteers and attendees at events explicitly requested that the campaign open an office in their area, anticipating the benefits not only to the candidate but to their own impending advocacy. For O'Neill, the requests started as soon as Trump's first office opened in New Hampshire in 2020.

> Manchester was our first office, so there were a lot of people that were excited. There were probably at least 100 people who came to our office opening and there was so much excitement. And for all of my volunteers, they came to me, and they asked me, "when are we going to get [an office]?" And so that was kind of the conversation of, "Okay, we wanted to do this, the

campaign itself wanted to do this, our volunteers want to do this. Let's find out where this will be, when it will be, and so on and so forth." (O'Neill, personal communication, August 2, 2022)

Opening a field office was perceived as a reward by volunteers and staff alike. The office became an outlet for people seeking a place to pick up campaign signs, buttons, and stickers, share some free food, or to even watch a nonpolitical sporting event. These sorts of effects are difficult to measure in the final vote count but important to campaigns trying to keep staff happy and volunteers engaged.

2.5 A Theory of Field Office Value

Our review of the literature and conversations with campaign officials provide several reasons to believe that field offices hold value for presidential campaigns, with the caveat that many of those core functions are replaceable using rapidly evolving digital technology.

First, campaigns serve as the points of coordination for many of the evidence-based tactics pioneered by campaigns in recent years (Darr and Levendusky 2014). The construction of walk packets and call lists, the training to have positive conversations with voters, and recruiting the volunteer power to accomplish voter contact goals are all aided by the opening of a local field office. By localizing their operations and trainings, campaigns can mitigate the collective action problem inherent in political volunteering and use more effective local canvassers (Enos and Hersh 2015; Sinclair et al. 2013).

Second, field offices serve as the inflection point for data collection and data usage. Individual-level data on how voters are feeling, whether they are registered, making sure they have a plan to vote, if they have moved: all of this can be collected reliably by volunteers at the doors and on the phones. Without up-to-date information on how voters are responding to campaign messages and feeling sufficiently motivated to vote, even the best statistical models in the world will have flaws: garbage in, garbage out, as they say. The data *collection* function of the work being done in these offices is easy to overlook compared to the data used to contact voters but is highly valuable to data-focused campaigns. Cabrera explained how this process worked for the Trump campaign in 2020:

> You need a good CRM (constituent relationship management) system, which we had, where data goes up and down, right? We input data from what we do in the field, and then they, you know, it comes down to us from folks that sign up, whether it be from a fundraising email from attending a rally to whatever else it may be. There's all sorts of sources that would come over to us, so I think it was a pipeline that went both ways. (Cabrera, personal communication, July 18, 2022)

Finally, field offices may be most valuable for harder-to-measure contributions to staff, volunteer, and supporter morale. Instead of relying upon robust local parties, unions, and third-party funding, recent campaigns have taken on these tasks in-house and must keep their new hires and fresh volunteers happy. In-person contact with like-minded coworkers and volunteers provides campaign staff with the purposive and solidary rewards that make them want to continue to engage in costly forms of participation. Campaigns also believe in the positive side of volunteer interactions, and encourage people to get personal:

> We always incorporated what I thought was best, making sure the volunteers are sharing any sort of anecdotal stories that they had as to why they were supporting President Trump. I think that's always helpful because it helps humanize the reason as to why somebody is doing something, and it's a very compelling message when you have somebody giving a personal anecdote as to why they are supporting or why they are volunteering. (Cabrera, personal communication, July 18, 2022)

Campaigns should (and, by and large, do) recognize the value of opening storefront offices across the nation in the spots they determine to be strategically valuable to cultivate local volunteers and make personal connections with voters and staffers. The next sections examine which areas receive these offices and whether they make a difference, to the extent we can answer those questions.

3 Placing Offices

Iowa City, Iowa, is exactly where one would expect a Democratic candidate to set up shop. As the home of the University of Iowa, its highly educated employees, and a population of younger, left-leaning college students, Democrats looking to win caucus delegates cannot ignore Iowa City or the rest of Johnson County, the most consistently liberal county in the state. Biden would eventually win Johnson County in 2020 with over 70 percent of the vote. Within the city, however, office locations and their uses varied wildly between the Democratic contenders.

A mile south of downtown, the Elizabeth Warren office at 322 East Second Street sat in a nondescript, brown-brick, red-roofed, single-floor, aging office park. It was divided into two rooms: the crowded entrance area with a reception desk, and the garage (for lack of a better word) in the back. The office had ample parking and space for trainings, gatherings, and casual workspace, but no windows and a distinctly "auto mechanic" aesthetic. This was an office in the sense that it had four walls and a roof, but lacked other amenities for volunteers, a sign on the door advertising its presence, or an accessible location for walking pedestrians.

A mile to the north up South Gilbert Street, the major road running past the Warren office's small side street, the brand-new Pete Buttigieg campaign office smelled like new paint. A big blue sign hung from the wall and a hand-written poster outside welcomed people in. Located directly across the street from city hall and a five-minute walk to the University of Iowa campus, the office was clearly geared toward young voters and would-be volunteers. The former tanning salon was covered in yellow-and-blue murals and featured a "selfie room" covered in *PETE* signs and a disco ball hanging from the ceiling.

Volunteers in both offices seemed happy and motivated. While it is tough to say which of these campaigns' offices was more effective at mobilizing voters, the strategic differences in their placement and the relative financial investment behind each were clear. Buttigieg's campaign wanted an office that was accessible to campus and attractive to students and passersby, while Warren was looking for the most space for their dollar to house their motivated volunteers who took the effort to drive there, get trained, and contact voters.

In this section, we examine the correlates and determinants of field office placement within states and cities. Campaigns looking to maximize their return on investment must choose where to invest in rent and staff to help generate the most volunteer activity and voter contact on their behalf. We examine campaign strategy using an original dataset of campaign field office locations in 2012, 2016, and 2020.

We begin by discussing placement strategies within battleground states in the 2012, 2016, and 2020 elections, followed by the first examination in the literature on field offices of placement strategies within metropolitan areas. Using analyses based on county-level statistics and interviews with some of the field staffers making these decisions, we attempt to determine not only what factors predict the presence of a field office, but also whether there are partisan differences and if strategies have changed over time. We pay particular attention to 2020, when the Trump campaign lacked a previously crucial factor for determining office placement: competition. By understanding the considerations behind where field offices are placed, we can better understand whether they have effects on voters and election outcomes.

3.1 Placement Considerations

Presidential campaigns are technically national but only actively contested in a shifting set of strategically determined battleground states (Shaw 2006). Over the period we measure, campaigns occasionally set up offices in non-battleground states, but rarely more than one or two per state, and usually as a base for fundraising, converting safe state volunteers into battleground state phone calls and canvassing trips, or as an investment in the future if a state's politics is heading in the party's direction (Darr and Levendusky 2014). Campaigns locate offices within battleground states to increase their chances of winning the election with 270 electoral votes.

Within battlegrounds, populations are not distributed evenly either in terms of population density or political preferences. In general, presidential elections in recent years have seen improving Republican performance in the rural areas of battleground states and Democratic strengths in cities and the suburbs, where Donald Trump tended to underperform previous Republican nominees. This geographic disparity, combined with the realities of the work of field offices and the utility of opening a storefront in a community, presents the two parties with different challenges and considerations for office placement.

Since Republicans' base of support is located within rural, exurban, and suburban communities, they face a different set of geographic challenges than Democrats do when attempting place-based mobilization. Houses are farther apart from each other, volunteers will need to drive to the office and park, and a lower population may mean a lower return on investment: while the whole of a state's rural population is a substantial electoral asset, each individual rural county contains relatively few voters in a place that is, by definition, a difficult place to knock doors. Campaigns may want to place offices in rural areas, and they may have more power to win votes in small towns, as a senior Democrat explained to us.

> You look at rural areas, and sometimes you can open one office and that'll just win it for you. It might not even be that active, maybe it's just a temporary office space, but a home for the people that want to get involved there to get involved on a regular basis. (senior Democrat, personal communication, September 1, 2022)

Republicans aiming to win rural votes still need to consider population, however. In New Hampshire, the northernmost county in the state, Coos County, is a prime example of this paradox. Until 2020, no Democrat had ever won the presidency without winning Coos County. Trump won the county 52 percent to 46 percent, a smaller margin than his 50 percent to 42 percent win in 2016. Coos, however, has very few residents: the final vote tally in 2020 was 8,617 for Trump to 7,640 for Biden. Trump went on to lose the state by 59,267 votes, roughly double the total population of Coos County, out of over 800,000 votes cast and his campaign rightly looked to other areas of the state to maximize the impact of their offices.

> I know that we had one in Rochester, we had one in Derry, we got one in Portsmouth, one in Manchester, and Nashua, a couple other locations as well,

but we didn't really have many in the northern part of the state because that's not where a lot of the population is. So it was a conversation with the campaign manager and the New Hampshire State Director was their official title and our field staff to kind of figure out which towns and which areas would work best to get more volunteers, more activists, anybody who wanted to be interested in helping with the campaign. (O'Neill, personal communication, August 2, 2022)

O'Neill's quote illustrates the Republican conundrum with field offices: the areas of battleground states that are moving in their direction and could benefit from some organizing are often too small to make a field investment worthwhile.

Democrats, on the other hand, face strong incentives to open offices within densely populated areas of cities. In these walkable neighborhoods divided into apartment buildings, or multi-family homes, volunteers may be able to knock many doors efficiently by walking and may not require an office with parking. However, it may also be more difficult to maintain reliable voter lists in places with a younger population that moves around more frequently and may not have landline telephones.

There is a matter of need: there are some areas, very Democratic areas, that have a lot of support, a lot of prospective people to mobilize to take action. So that place is probably smart for you to put a field office, for all of those people to be able to take action in this area, to allow you to harness all of that activity. (senior Democrat, personal communication, September 1, 2022)

Finding your supporters is not enough: campaigns must also avoid mobilizing their opponent's voters, and campaign activities can have this backlash effect (Bailey et al. 2016; Chen and Reeves 2011; Heersink et al. 2021). Well-maintained and accurate voter lists are essential for mobilization efforts for this reason, and the quality and price of these lists varies wildly between states (Hersh 2015). Campaigns may not want to risk talking to everyone they come across and selectively adopting persuasion appeals for undecided or opposition voters and mobilization appeals for supporters. Attempts at persuasion, even when conducted using the effective mobilization tactic of canvassing, can backfire and reduce candidate support (Bailey et al. 2016).

Campaigns may recognize these limitations of persuasion and locate offices in areas of strength while avoiding contested or opposition counties, unless they have enough confidence in their voter data to find and mobilize their voters even where they are not plentiful (Issenberg 2012). As such, there are positives and negatives to organizing the areas of strength for each party before even considering the question of within-area competition. Campaigns may feel the need to "match" their opponent's investment, particularly within swing counties, so as not to cede these tossup areas (Darr and Levendusky 2014; Masket et al. 2016).

These decisions require both anticipation and reaction: campaigns must consider where to open offices early in the campaign at the same time that their opponent is making those decisions. Field offices require space rental and establishing a community of organizers and volunteers to be most effective. There is no equivalent of a last second ad buy where more recent exposure to the campaign treatment may be more effective (Hill et al. 2013), or a final trip to a crucial area by the candidate themselves to generate enthusiasm and earned media, when it comes to mobilizing voters through personal contact. Campaigns therefore must choose where to compete before the campaign gets into its final stretch.

3.2 Data Collection

Campaigns do not necessarily make it easy for interested researchers, reporters, or members of the public to find their field office locations online. Reporters may be forced to rely upon campaigns to publicize their own voter contact operations – the organizational equivalent of an internal poll – while forcing volunteers to enter their personal information online before volunteering. Our data collection needed to draw from a variety of sources and approaches, and include latitude and longitude while also grouping each office into the county it served.

Data on field offices was collected using both primary and secondary sources from 2012 to the present. Data from past elections, 2004 and 2008, was collected from Democracy in Action, a comprehensive resource of campaign staff and organization maintained by Eric Appleman and hosted by George Washington University (Darr and Levendusky 2014; Masket 2009). Subsequent elections were collected from the candidate websites themselves over the course of the election by Darr and research assistants in 2012, 2016, and 2020. In 2012, both candidates listed their offices on their websites. 2016 proved the most challenging: the candidates put their office locations either in events maps (Trump) or accessible by entering one's ZIP code (Clinton). These office locations were obtained through consistent observation and systematic ZIP code entry. In 2020, Trump's office locations were once again collected using the events map hosted by Trump Victory.

These inconsistent and secretive practices by campaigns are barriers to transparency and political participation, and the difficulty of collecting data disincentivizes reporters from reporting on the totality of field operations. Greater transparency about office locations would help potential volunteers participate and empower future research into this question.

3.3 Placing Offices within States

Though some last longer than others, there are no permanent battleground states. The two states that decided the 2000 and 2004 presidential elections,

Florida and Ohio, respectively, tipped decisively into the Republican column in 2016 and 2020 when Donald Trump was the Republican nominee. On the other side, Arizona and Georgia became battlegrounds and flipped from Trump in 2016 to Biden in 2020 after being lightly contested in previous elections. The regular battlegrounds of Wisconsin and Pennsylvania featured particularly prominently in 2016 and 2020: their flip to Trump in 2016 arguably delivered him the election (along with Michigan), and their swing back to the Democratic column in 2020 powered Biden's victory without needing Florida and Ohio.

Since Arizona and Georgia emerged as battlegrounds in 2020, when Biden's campaign did not open field offices, we will concentrate on the fading battlegrounds of Florida and Ohio and the most important states in 2016 and 2020, Wisconsin and Pennsylvania. These states all contain major cities and large rural areas, and the Democratic and Republican campaigns faced many of the considerations outlined above as they made their decisions.

Florida, the quintessential battleground state since Tim Russert's famous whiteboard proclamation of "Florida, Florida, Florida" on Election Night 2000, received substantial investments in each of the three cycles measured (Figure 2). The eventual winner of the state in 2012, Barack Obama, opened 103 offices compared to Romney's 46. Obama's offices were distributed across all areas of the state, including dense investments in the Miami – Fort Lauderdale area, Jacksonville, and the Tampa Bay area down the coast into Fort Myers. Romney opened similar numbers of offices in core Republican and swing counties across the state while investing less in Democratic areas, while Obama invested deeply in core Democratic areas such as Orlando and Miami and in swing and core Republican areas (Darr and Levendusky 2014). With more than double Romney's offices and a superior data operation (Issenberg 2012), Obama's campaign could target swing and opponent areas more effectively while running up the score in their core counties.

In 2016, Florida received far less attention from the Clinton and Trump campaigns: Clinton opened only sixty-eight offices, while Trump's twenty-two offices were less than half of Romney's total. This drop appears to have come from the Tampa area, where Trump barely invested (three offices), the rural/exurban counties in the north around Gainesville and Ocala, and the Atlantic coast north of West Palm Beach. There was also far less investment in right-leaning Sarasota, Charlotte, and Lee counties between Sarasota and Fort Myers on the Gulf side.

Republican investment bounced back to 2012 levels in 2020, as Trump opened forty-three offices. Trump outdid Romney's investment in the northern-central areas of the state surrounding Ocala, including Putnam County (population 73,300) and Citrus County (153,800), which did not have offices from any campaign in 2012 or 2016. Trump won each county with around 70 percent of

2012

✕ Romney ● Obama

2016

✕ Trump ● Clinton

2020

✕ Trump

Figure 2 Democratic and Republican field offices in Florida, 2012, 2016, and 2020

the vote, and improved upon his 2016 totals in each. While Trump did not reach Obama's levels of total offices, he pursued a base activation strategy that reflected his strength in the state. If anything, given his 3.5 percent margin of victory, Trump may have overinvested in the Sunshine State relative to some closer battlegrounds such as Georgia and Arizona.

In the Buckeye State (Figure 3), waning Democratic strength in 2016 precipitated Trump's near-ignoring of the state in 2020. No battleground state shifted more decisively right between 2012 and 2016 than Ohio, but the 2016 Clinton campaign treated the state like it was still neck-and-neck.

The 2012 Obama campaign opened 131 offices in Ohio, the most of any state. They were determined to find voters everywhere they could, including targeting smaller black populations in majority-white counties with small cities. Obama field organizer Addisu Demissie explained the strategy in a 2012 article for *The Grio*:

> I remember one story – perhaps apocryphal, but certainly illustrative – of field organizers in 2008 who knocked on doors in heavily black neighborhoods in Lima (Allen County had gone 66–34 for Bush in 2004) that had literally never been canvassed before. The 2008 campaign understood that an Obama vote in Lima was just as valuable as one in Cleveland. And so while we still lost those counties, we lost by less – 20 points instead of 30 in Allen and Butler, 10 instead of 20 in Marion, and so on. (Demissie 2012)

This strategy was not evident in 2016, when the Clinton campaign opened far fewer offices in the western half of the state. Even in 2008, in Demissie's accounting, Obama did not improve on Kerry's margin in Cleveland, winning instead by finding votes elsewhere. Clinton's offices in the eastern half of the state ran headfirst into Trump's considerable appeal in Appalachia. By 2020, Trump only opened eight offices in the state on his way to winning it by eight points. If Democrats are to seriously contend for Ohio in the future – and it may not be worth the expense, if current trends endure – they should return to the surgical approach of the Obama years.

Wisconsin (Figure 4) was decided by less than one percent and roughly 20,000 votes in each of the 2016 and 2020 elections following a comfortable seven-point Obama win in 2012. Obama invested heavily in the state in 2012, with sixty-nine offices compared to Romney's twenty-three. These offices were concentrated in the Milwaukee and Madison areas, but also spread out across the more rural areas in the northern part of the state where Obama was less popular (Cramer 2016). Trump's win in the state in 2016 illustrated the enormity of the midwestern shift away from Democrats, particularly in rural communities. Clinton's campaign opened forty offices, with weaker investment in Democratic core areas and fewer offices up north and in the state's southwestern counties.

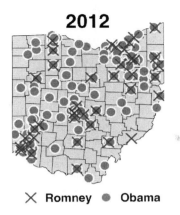

2012

✕ Romney ● Obama

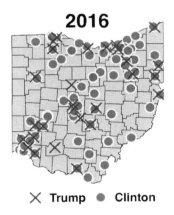

2016

✕ Trump ● Clinton

2020

✕ Trump

Figure 3 Democratic and Republican field offices in Ohio, 2012, 2016, and 2020

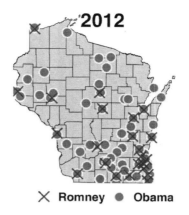

X Romney ● Obama

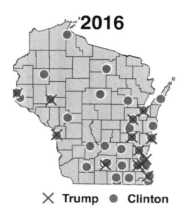

X Trump ● Clinton

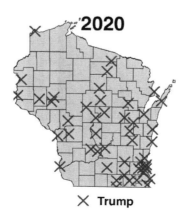

X Trump

Figure 4 Democratic and Republican field offices in Wisconsin, 2012, 2016, and 2020

Trump invested heavily in Wisconsin in 2020, opening fifty offices across the state – one of the few instances where Trump 2020 had more offices than Clinton 2016. This included offices in counties that were ignored in 2012 and 2016. Small towns like Sparta (population 10,025) and Chippewa Falls (14,800) in Monroe and Chippewa counties, respectively, each received a 2020 office and shifted from roughly 50–50 in 2012 to 60–40 Trump in 2020. As in Florida, Trump's field operation targeted counties that were shifting in his direction to consolidate those gains, though it was not enough to win the state.

In Pennsylvania (Figure 5), Clinton's field team opened more offices (57) than Obama did in 2012 (54), a rarity across most states. Trump's appeal in Appalachia opened the door to his 2016 victory, despite a light investment of eleven offices, before barely losing by 1.2 percent in 2020. Clinton may have miscalculated in 2016 by investing more heavily in the central part of the state than Obama did. For example, Obama's campaign did not have an office in Elk, Clearfield, or Indiana counties, but Clinton invested there despite losing those counties by 42, 49, and 35 percent, respectively. Unlike in Ohio, where there were votes to earn in small cities like Lima, these counties each contained 1.5 percent or fewer African-American voters. With so little base to mobilize, Clinton's efforts were at best inefficient, and at worst may have backfired.

Trump's campaign recognized the importance of defending the state in 2020 and quadrupled their investment to forty-four offices. Many of these offices went to the Philadelphia and Pittsburgh suburbs, as was common across years, but Trump also clearly tried to open offices in central and northwest Pennsylvania. Though these counties were very friendly to Trump's message, their population is miniscule relative to the rest of the state: in Clearfield and Indiana counties, which switched from uncontested Clinton offices in 2016 to Trump in 2020, only about 40,000 people voted in 2020.

Taken together, these state-level trends across elections are instructive about the changing contours of American politics and campaigns' strategic responses. Trump's campaign recognized the importance of rural voters for their chances but faced a ceiling of potential impact due to the small populations of those areas. Within major cities, Democrats consistently open more offices than Republicans, but their success in less-urban areas may depend upon whether they have the data and resources to locate friendly voters in opposition strongholds.

3.4 Placing Offices within Metropolitan Areas

Within population centers, some areas may be more or less friendly to campaigns but most are worth organizing due to the sheer number of voters. Democrats have a natural advantage in cities, but Republicans cannot concede

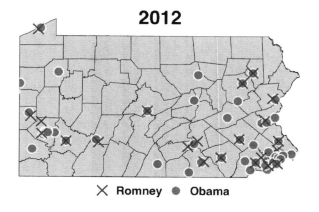

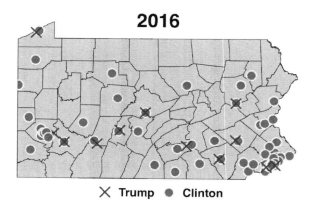

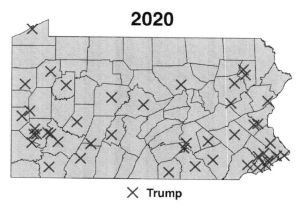

Figure 5 Democratic and Republican field offices in Pennsylvania, 2012, 2016, and 2020

them entirely. In 2020, with Democrats off the "field," the door was open for Trump's campaign to locate and organize his voters within larger metropolitan areas. This section presents the first scholarly analysis of patterns of within-city office placement across multiple metropolitan areas (though see the map of Cincinnati in Masket et al. 2016), starting in a state where one city defines the contest: Nevada.

From the perspective of political campaigns, the state is composed of Las Vegas and everywhere else. Nearly three out of every four Nevadans live in Clark County, making it the key to the state's six electoral votes. The tourist capital also has several features that affect organizing, which a senior Democratic organizer (see Section 2) described to us. He singled out East Las Vegas, in particular, as a difficult but essential place to organize and win.

> You have some circumstances where [opening an office] may be needed, not necessarily from a perspective of we have a lot of volunteers here, but it makes it easier to get volunteers here. For example, Las Vegas, the east side of Las Vegas. That is the reason Hillary Clinton won the primary there in 2016, it is the reason why Barack Obama won that state in 2012. It is a majority Latino community, it is hard to organize. I would say it's arguably one of the hardest places to organize in the country. For many reasons: one, Las Vegas is a super transient place, so there's a little bit of a lack of community, no one knows each other. We're talking about a community, you know, that there are a lot of mixed-status households: so someone knocking on the door with a clipboard, they're not like "Come on in!" There's a lot of reasons why it's tough to organize. So our strategy there, to make it easier for folks to get involved, is to blanket the place with offices so that there's one in walking distance in a community where a lot of the people we want to volunteer may not have cars, or may not have public transportation. So there's that need: we really need to organize this area, it's really tough for the people we need to take action, they can't just drive 20 minutes to an office – how about we make sure that we have an office within a half mile. (senior Democrat, personal communication, September 1, 2022)

Democrats' focus on East Las Vegas was clear in 2012, when the area was blanketed in offices (Figure 6). This election provided the best example of our interviewee's point: Obama's campaign made sure it got the most out of the most difficult area to organize, where there was no substitute for a widespread presence: the twenty-one offices in Clark County were by far his most in any single county in the nation. Romney did not compete much in the city, locating four of his five offices on the outskirts of town. Even in those areas, however, Obama matched him, locating offices practically next to Romney's in the Spring Valley and Green Valley areas south of downtown.

Clinton's ten offices in 2016 were also among her highest number anywhere but represented less than half of Obama's offices and particularly ignored East

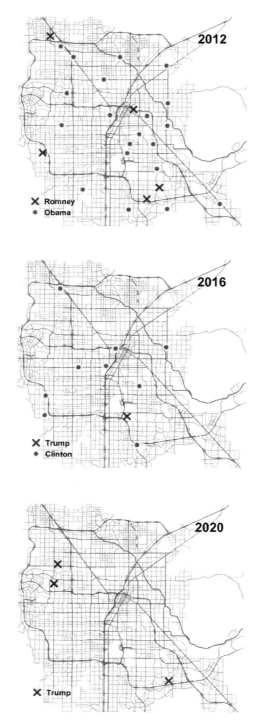

Figure 6 Democratic and Republican field offices in Las Vegas, Nevada, 2012, 2016, and 2020

Las Vegas, the area identified by our interviewee as the most valuable place for storefront offices. Trump Victory only opened one office, notably located south of the Strip and not in the Trump International Hotel. While Clinton won the state, there was noticeably less organization in Clark County across both campaigns in 2016 than in 2012. Trump was even less aggressive in 2020: he opened only three offices, none of which were in East Las Vegas. When Democrats are not competing in their areas of strength, it seems that Republicans will not necessarily come rushing in.

Not all battleground state cities show this same drop-off between cycles. The Miami-Ft. Lauderdale area, a treasure trove of votes in the perennial swing state of Florida, presents an example with very little drop-off on either side between 2012 and 2020 and little change in Republican strategy in 2020. The metropolitan area mapped in Figure 7, from south of Miami north through Ft. Lauderdale, shows continued and sustained investment by the Clinton campaign in 2016 after a wide and deep Obama presence in 2012: nine offices compared to Obama's thirteen. There are few differences: for example, Obama located two offices in North Miami while Clinton had none, as well as one in Miami Beach that Clinton did not repeat (in what must have been a crushing blow to her organizing staff). Romney had only seven offices to Trump's five, so neither Democrat was in danger of falling behind their opponent.

In 2020, Trump's campaign once again only opened five offices, but overperformed in Miami-Dade relative to recent Republicans. In 2004, George

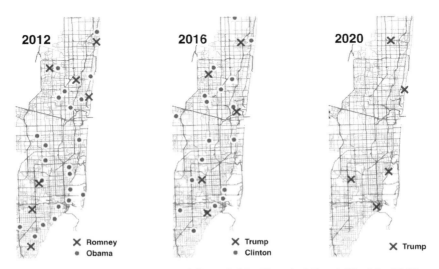

Figure 7 Democratic and Republican field offices in Miami, Florida, 2012, 2016, and 2020

W. Bush won 46.6 percent of the vote in Miami-Dade, but McCain's total dropped to 41.7 percent, Romney dropped further to 37.9 percent, and Trump cratered in 2016 at 33.8 percent. In 2020, that trend reversed sharply, bouncing back up to Bush-like levels of 46 percent. Whatever the reasons for Trump's stronger showing – tougher policies toward Cuba, or success tying Biden's campaign to the concept of "socialism" (Sesin 2020) – it was not due to deeper investment in the field than his predecessors. Whether or not Miami receives field resources in future cycles from either party may depend upon whether Trump is the nominee.

In a state that will unquestionably be hotly contested in 2024 and beyond, Wisconsin, the largest trove of votes can be found in the Milwaukee area (Figure 8). If Republicans lose the suburbs, they face steep odds statewide, and Democrats are in trouble if they cannot get the votes they need from the city. The year 2012 illustrates this traditional divide nicely: Romney's offices are firmly in the suburbs (Fox Point to the north, Wauwatosa and West Allis to the West), while Obama's are concentrated downtown and spread out into the northeast of the county. In 2016, when she narrowly lost the state, Clinton's campaign reduced their investment to three offices surrounding downtown (compared to Obama's two located in the middle of it), and overall opened four offices in the county compared to Obama's eleven. Trump's campaign also avoided downtown in 2016, when turnout was somewhat lower (and third-party vote share higher).

In 2020, Trump moved in, unlike in Miami or Las Vegas. Trump opened five offices in the county, including two downtown – a first for Republicans over these cycles. His office at 2244 North Martin Luther King Drive – five blocks from Clinton's 2016 office at 2701 North Martin Luther King Drive – was specifically designated a "Black Voices for Trump Office" by the campaign and is located in Milwaukee's historically African-American neighborhood of Bronzeville.

This office was opened by the state party in February 2020 and explicitly touted as the first Republican field office in Milwaukee. At the opening, attended by around seventy-five people, Senator Ron Johnson spoke about the party's "very genuine and sincere effort asking people to just listen to us, to just consider a different approach," and Milwaukee Republicans expressed some hope about the impact of an office: "I hope they're seeing we want to get involved with this office. Not sitting on the outside and saying, 'We're here, now vote for us'" (Hess 2020).

Democrats were not convinced: after the opening, a party spokesman replied, "If (the Wisconsin GOP) wants to light a pile of money on fire by foolishly trying to trick Milwaukee area voters, that's their decision" (Hess 2020). The GOP also opened a "Latinos for Trump Office" at 725 West Historic Mitchell Street on the city's South Side, just four blocks from Clinton's 2016 office at

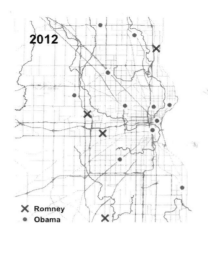

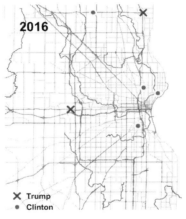

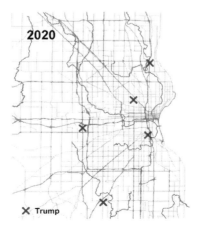

Figure 8 Democratic and Republican field offices in Milwaukee, Wisconsin, 2012, 2016, and 2020

1107. Investing in racially and ethnically distinct neighborhoods was intended to be a signal from campaigns that they take those votes seriously, and Trump's 2020 campaign was the first Republican effort in recent cycles to do so.

The campaign may have been onto something: though Trump lost the state, his share of votes in the city of Milwaukee stayed roughly stable from 2016 to 2020 (19.3 vs. 19.9 percent; Habeck 2020), though it should be noted that his vote share increased in many large cities across the country without any campaign activity. It was the suburbs, ironically, where Trump lost significant ground. In the Fox Point area north of downtown, Trump received 29 percent of the vote, down from 33.8 in 2016; he fell a similar four points, from 48.4 to 44.4 percent, in West Allis; and in Wauwatosa, his vote share fell from 38.1 percent in 2016 to 32.6 percent in 2020. All these towns experienced higher turnout in 2020 than in 2016, and these losses added up: two towns in Milwaukee County, Greenfield and Greendale (where Trump did have an office), flipped from Trump in 2016 to Biden in 2020.

Philadelphia (Figure 9) is another large city in a critical 2020 swing state with traditionally competitive suburbs. Trump subtly shifted strategy in 2020 without a Democratic opponent to compete against. In previous cycles, Democrats dominated the city while Republicans set up outposts in the farther-flung suburbs, though as usual Obama (12) outdid Clinton (8) in the city. Trump barely opened offices at all, with only two (including one downtown) in the area in 2016. Trump's 2020 campaign opened another Black Voices for Trump office in West Philadelphia at 5558 Chestnut Street, as well as an office in Northwest Philadelphia. Other than that, the suburban patterns are nearly identical to Romney's, spread out across Delaware, Montgomery, and Bucks counties. Biden improved over Clinton's margin by three or four points in each of these counties.

The trend by Trump and the GOP to open offices in racially and ethnically distinct neighborhoods is worth watching in 2024 and beyond. Mathematically, shifts in the suburbs ended up being more consequential than those cities in the battleground states that mattered most (Frey 2020). Trump Victory's commitment to storefront campaigning in 2020, which exceeded any previous Republicans', was impressive. But it did not reach Obama-level saturation in these states, where they spent the resources to invest in cities and suburbs and rural areas alike. Trump's campaign lost the states that delivered them the win in 2016, despite an influx of field offices distributed across the states responsible for his victory.

3.5 Predicting Placement across Cycles

While these conclusions about the geography of field strategy are largely interpretive, they help illustrate the promise and the difficulties of predicting where field offices will be needed months in advance. Campaign strategies are

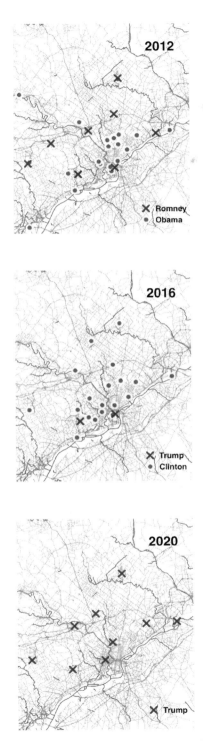

Figure 9 Democratic and Republican field offices in Philadelphia, Pennsylvania, 2012, 2016, and 2020

limited by the rent they are willing and able to pay, their resources for recruiting volunteers, and their belief in the power of person-to-person communication relative to digital outreach or advertisements. The factors leading to the opening of a field office may be specific to each party, to each candidate's individual philosophy, or an interaction of the two.

The organizers we talked to explained some of these considerations in greater detail, particularly when it came to publicizing the opening and activities in those centers. Peter O'Neill, the Republican organizing staffer in New Hampshire, described the "double edged sword" of operating in closely contested areas or those where opponents are strong:

> We want everybody who wants to be there to be able to be there, but we also don't want a bunch of protesters to show up and people to create mischief. So yes, we did advertise [the office opening], but it was more so in local GOP circles, we didn't send it out on Twitter, we didn't have a gigantic email blast. It was something that we wanted to have it out in people's circles and in the back of their minds, like hey our office opening is coming up, but we didn't want that to be super public knowledge, so we're kind of straddling that line. (O'Neill, personal communication, August 2, 2022)

How partisans and opponents will react is clearly at the top of organizers' minds. Can we discern some of the broader dynamics of field office placement in the data, and are there within-party or across-party trends across elections? Darr and Levendusky (2014) create a model of field office placement that tested three possible influences on geographic strategies for field in the 2012 election: partisan vote of the county; "swing" counties that are closely contested and "core" counties that their party regularly wins; and "matching" their opponent's offices strategically by avoiding opponents' core counties and defending swing counties.

The authors found that both Obama and Romney tended to open offices in the same counties and those with a favorable partisan lean (Darr and Levendusky 2014). There were also some differences between parties: Romney's campaign invested roughly equally in swing and core areas, while Obama's campaign focused more strongly on core Democratic counties. Obama did not "match" Romney's investments in swing counties or Republican-leaning counties and invested less in these unfavorable areas.[2] Romney, on the other hand, was more likely to invest in swing counties where Obama offices were located, but also avoided significant investments in Democratic counties with Obama offices.

---

[2] A notable result, to the point by Addisu Demissie quoted earlier: the only model in which "percent African-American" is positive and significant is Column 5 in Table 1 (p. 535), hinting at the strategy he describes from 2012 of finding African-American voters in otherwise unfavorable counties. In Darr (2020), regarding the 2016 election, the corresponding coefficient for percent African-American is not significant.

Darr (2020) updated this analysis using data from 2016 and found similar trends to 2012 in the Trump-Clinton contest. The findings that diverge from 2012's strategies show that the candidates were more timid in 2016, or found other uses for their funds: either way, Trump was less likely to invest in swing counties (with or without Clinton offices), and Clinton was less likely to open offices in Republican counties. While the candidates were still more likely to open offices where their opponent did, all the coefficients were smaller due to the much smaller total number of offices.

Was there a noticeable change in strategy in 2020, when Trump's campaign was alone in the field, compared to 2016? We estimated the influences on office placement using a similar model as Darr and Levendusky (2014) and Darr (2020) about the 2012 and 2016 elections, respectively. The major change, of course, is that there is no variable for "opponent's field office." Covariates remained the same: battleground state status, median age, population and population squared, median income, percent African-American, percent Hispanic, percent with less than a high school diploma, and percent with a college degree. We present these estimates alongside those from 2012 and 2016 in Figures 10, 11, and 12, with full results in the Online Appendix.

The unique circumstances of 2020 make it difficult to compare across years, given that the most consistent predictor of a campaign's field office placement is the location of their opponents' offices. Given that we now have three cycles of data with a roughly level financial playing field, however, it may be possible to discern partisan trends across time. In this section, we present the analyses described above (Darr 2020; Darr and Levendusky 2014) as more intuitive coefficient plots to show how Democrats and Republicans differed over time.

The most basic model from both previous articles examines Republican normal vote (Levendusky et al. 2008), calculated as the average of Republican presidential vote share in the community over the preceding three elections (i.e. Republican normal vote in 2020 is an average of 2008, 2012, and 2016). By estimating the enduring partisan tilt of a county, we can approximate how they are viewed in the eyes of those making placement decisions (Figure 10). Our dependent variable is measured here as the number of offices per county, giving a sense of not only whether a county received an office, but also how deep the investment was.

Viewed together, Democratic campaigns clearly avoided Republican-leaning counties far more than Republicans did. Obama's 2012 campaign invested least in Republican areas, though Clinton also stayed away. Romney in 2012 and Trump in 2016 each slightly favored more Republican areas, but in 2020 – with the entire field to himself – Trump's campaign was less aggressive about placing offices in Republican-leaning areas despite opening more total offices than

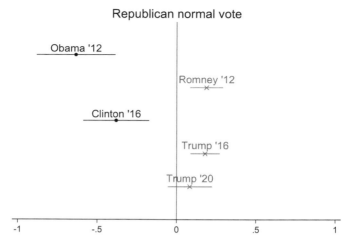

Figure 10 Estimated likelihood of Democratic and Republican field office placement by Republican normal vote, 2012, 2016, and 2020. Full results in Table A3.1 of the Online Appendix

either of the two preceding campaigns. This provides some evidence to bolster the idea that Trump attempted to broaden the playing field without competition from Biden, as seen in Milwaukee and Philadelphia above.

This finding comes at a time when base activation is increasingly the go-to strategy (Panagopoulos 2020). While recent research shows that independents are being left behind as campaigns bombard ideologues and strong partisans with specialized messages, there is a trend toward convergence in the aggregate partisanship of counties that receive campaigns' organizing resources.

What about the counties that swing back and forth between election cycles? There is some logic in tipping the most hotly contested areas in your favor, but areas with a more politically mixed electorate also pose the risk of accidentally activating opposing voters (Chen and Reeves 2011), and efforts at persuasion may be fraught compared to base activation (Bailey et al. 2016; Cox and McCubbins 1986). There are also geographic factors at play: swing counties tend to have smaller populations than core Democratic counties that Republicans wish to avoid, so the reward is smaller and the risk is higher. Figure 11 contains the results of analyses of placement by swing counties and core counties.

Figure 11 demonstrates that, in general, campaigns did not make a point of opening storefronts in swing counties. Only two campaigns invested significantly more in these areas, and the effects are small: Romney in 2012 and Trump in 2020. These are also the two campaigns that made the most serious Republican

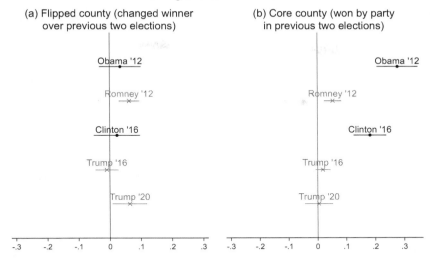

Figure 11 Estimated likelihood of Democratic and Republican field office placement in swing and core counties, 2012, 2016, and 2020. Full results in Table A3.2 of the Online Appendix

investments in storefront campaigning, with around 300 offices in both cases. Given their understandable aversion to mobilizing in Democratic core counties, and the possible diminishing returns of organizing more rural counties, Republicans are clearly in something of a bind. Romney's admirable field effort was significantly more invested in core counties, but neither Trump 2016 nor Trump 2020 gave more organizing resources to reliably Republican counties.

If the value of field offices is in running up the score with the base, Republicans may be at a structural disadvantage relative to Democrats: the average Democratic core county in 2020 was in the 32nd percentile, compared to the average Republican core county in the 53rd percentile. Swing counties were in the middle (42.5th percentile). This means more space between voters and heightened relevance for the saying, "land doesn't vote." The ceiling for total Republican offices may be structural as much as it is strategic, compared to Democrats' capacity to mobilize their densely packed troves of voters in battleground state cities.

3.6 Potential Moderators: Rurality, Ideology, Social Capital

Since the initial publication of Darr and Levendusky (2014), politics has changed and better county-level political data is available. In this section, we briefly update the findings above in light of three potentially impactful moderators: the rurality of a county, the county's aggregate estimated political ideology, and the baseline levels of social capital available in the county. Given the recent rural/urban polarization that defined the 2016 and 2020 elections, the improvements in measuring ideology beyond aggregated presidential results, and the need for campaigns to recruit active, quality volunteers, these new sources of data should help us better understand placement strategies. Each of these analyses uses the regression from Model 1, with the proposed moderator in place of the "Republican normal vote" variable.

3.6.1 Rurality

The political divide between urban and rural Americans defined the 2016 election: Trump's strength in rural areas fueled his victory in the midwestern "blue wall" states of Wisconsin, Michigan, and Pennsylvania (Scala and Johnson 2017). The growing political divide between big cities and less-populated rural areas should have clear implications for field organization decisions: if Democrats' dependence on maximizing votes from cities grows, so should their investments there. The Republican side is less clear: while the sum total of rural areas is a powerful electoral force, each individual rural county may lack the population to make a storefront presence efficient.

Rurality is measured by the Economic Research Service of the US Department of Agriculture, using a 1–9 scale (least to most rural). Each county is classified according to its degree of urbanization and closeness to a metropolitan area. In the analyses shown in panel (a) of Figure 12, the scale is recoded from 0 to 1. Since population is a covariate, these results should not be taken as an indication that campaigns invest equally in highly populated and less-populated areas. Instead, they compare across urban and rural areas holding other covariates constant, including highly correlated factors like population and income.

The results show that, in general, rurality is not a significant determinant of field office placement. Romney and Clinton show that offices are less likely to be found in rural areas, with the effect strongest for Clinton. While this relationship is not strong enough to explain Trump's decisive performance in rural areas, it is another example of Clinton's allocation decisions failing to anticipate how the race would shake out. At the same time, Trump did not invest more in rural areas in either 2016 or 2020 to accentuate his strengths in those areas.

3.6.2 County-Level Ideology

The placement analyses above showed the importance of county-level partisan vote share, measured as Republican normal vote (Levendusky et al. 2008), in determining which areas receive a field office. Since the initial analyses in Darr

Likelihood of an additional field office in county, by key moderators

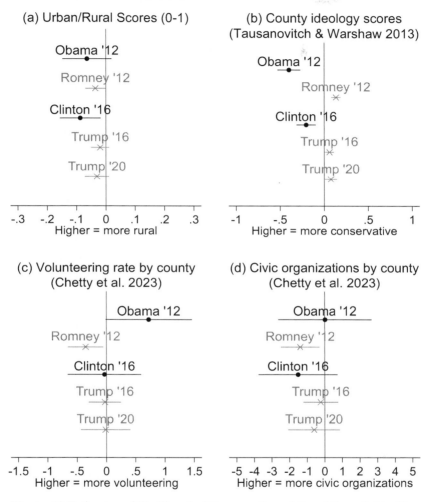

Figure 12 Estimates of likelihood of Democratic and Republican field office placement (a) in urban and rural counties, (b) by county ideology, (c) by county volunteering rate, and (d) by civic organizations per county, 2012, 2016, and 2020. Full results in Tables A3.3a, b, c, and d of the Online Appendix

and Levendusky (2014), several other ways to measure aggregated political preferences have emerged, including estimates of county-level ideology from the American Ideology Project (Tausanovitch and Warshaw 2014). These estimates should help confirm whether county ideology functions similarly to county partisanship.

Overall, the results presented in panel (b) of Figure 12 resemble those in Figure 11: county partisanship is a much more potent force for Democrats than for Republican candidates over these three cycles. Obama invested heavily in the most liberal counties, while Romney and (to an even lesser extent) both Trump campaigns were barely more likely to open offices in more conservative counties. If anything, Trump's 2016 campaign invested more in Republican counties than conservative ones, consistent with findings that he appealed to Republicans that were not as ideologically conservative (Sides, Tesler, and Vavreck 2018). In general, however, the main takeaway is the similarities between the influences of county-level partisanship and ideology.

3.6.3 Social Capital

Geographic density and political leanings alone do not provide the raw materials of storefront campaigning: campaigns need to recruit and train an active base of local, effective volunteers to send out to the doors and work the phones (Sinclair et al. 2013). Political scientists have found that, while not entirely dependent upon socio-economic status (SES), volunteerism and participation in civic organizations relies upon individual-level resources such as money, time, and skills (Verba et al. 1995). Participation in church groups or employment at a job where outreach and public speaking are required, not merely their income, education, or status, helps people build civic skills. As such, county-level differences in the opportunities to participate should be impactful and capture more than income or educational variation. Recent scholarship by economist Raj Chetty and others attempts to measure reservoirs of social capital by county using data from 21 billion Facebook friendships (Chetty et al. 2022).

We use two measures from Chetty et al. (2022), volunteering rates and the density of civic organizations within counties.[3] If campaigns open more offices in areas with higher volunteering rates or more civic organizations, it could demonstrate that they are attuned to the "supply" of the resources they hope to exploit: committed, experienced, and reliable volunteers. Results are shown in panels (c) and (d) of Figure 12.

Our analyses do not find meaningful effects of the "raw materials" of organizing in the calculus of field office placement, with some exceptions. Obama 2012 seems to have invested substantially more in areas with high levels of volunteerism, though the confidence interval is quite wide. Across

---

[3] Chetty et al. (2022) define volunteering rates as the share of Facebook users in an area who are a member of at least one volunteering or activism group, defined by a set of the fifty largest national volunteering organizations and the largest in each state. Civic organizations per county are categorized according to the "public good" designation on Facebook, limited to those with websites and/or descriptions on their Facebook pages.

both variables, Romney 2012 was significantly less likely to open offices in areas with higher volunteering rates and civic organizations, while the rest of the campaigns in 2016 and 2020 showed no effects of these variables. Obama's broader reach in 2012 may explain this variation, and the results suggest that this broader strategy may have helped his campaign locate areas with more volunteerism (if not areas with more civic organizations, for which the coefficient was almost exactly zero). While the supply of experienced volunteers could help a campaign recruit, that quantity may not be apparent enough to influence campaigns' office placement decisions.

These recently available moderating variables allowed us to test some alternative influences on office placement, but ultimately reaffirmed that partisan composition of a county is the most important factor. The campaign with the most offices in our sample, Obama 2012, was also the only campaign to invest in counties with more volunteerism and the campaign with the most investments in ideologically friendly (liberal, in this case) counties. More offices suggests that the campaign was willing and able to take chances targeting potentially favorable but previously ignored populations (Demissie 2012) or broaden coalitions through racially and ethnically targeted offices, as Trump did in 2020 in Milwaukee and Philadelphia.

3.7 Conclusion

Democrats and Republicans face fundamentally different challenges when deciding where to open field offices. Democrats may have an easier time using volunteers to reach voters, but their voter-rich urban base of support may have a ceiling. Republicans have a tougher time mobilizing enough support from rural counties to counterbalance Democrats' advantages and have seen their suburban support slip even as they make inroads into majority-minority neighborhoods.

We still have not seen a Republican investment in field organization on the scale of Obama's 2012 campaign or even Clinton's considerably smaller 2016 operation. Short of an incredibly expensive distribution of offices across swing state rural counties – there are thirty-six counties in Wisconsin alone that are over 99 percent rural, according to the Census Bureau (Stacker 2022) – it is unclear where these offices might go. In the future, Republicans could continue Trump's efforts to chip away at Democratic support within cities, but may find themselves disadvantaged without a corresponding defense of the suburbs.

Regardless of effects, observations of campaigns' field office placement can give observers (and their opponents) insight into their perceived path to victory and strategic assessments. Advertising is a crude way to assess targeting since ad buys must be made within geographically constrained areas across county and state lines. Candidate appearances can be adjusted somewhat quickly to seize upon last-minute opportunities, as with Mitt Romney's last-minute Pennsylvania appearances and advertising blitz in 2012. Renting and staffing storefronts, however, can reveal the campaign's theory of the race from the beginning. the next section, we will explore whether these offices can achieve their goals of increased turnout and partisan vote share and the factors that may moderate those effects.

4 Ground Gains

Campaigns love to brag about how many doors they knocked, using big round numbers to earn glowing media coverage of their organizational prowess. In September 2020, for example, an article in POLITICO declared: "Trump's campaign knocks on a million doors a week. Biden's knocks on zero" (Thompson 2020). Axios reported in 2022 that, "The door wars are back: Minnesota candidates hit 1 million voter homes in battle for Capitol" (Van Oot 2022). Not to be outdone, in August 2022, Beto O'Rourke's campaign made a bold promise: "Beto O'Rourke campaign seeks to knock on 5 million doors before November election" (Mekelburg 2022).

The use of this metric can be deceiving, however. A door knocked is not the same as a conversation with a voter: many people are not home or unwilling to talk to a stranger about politics at their door. If campaigns knock on many doors from poorly tailored lists, they risk backlash from voters that are opposed or on the fence (Bailey et al. 2016). Regardless, reporters tend to be overly credulous about campaigns' broad and vague claims of dominance, innovation, and spending in the field.

For example, in an article about Florida Governor and 2024 presidential candidate Ron DeSantis' "$100 million field operation," one consultant boasted that "this is the most expansive, most in-depth, most cooperative, most intensive – fill in however many words you want to there that mean the same thing – program that I've ever seen" (Burns and Smith 2023). Despite the open invitation to use synonyms, the article does not present any evidence to support this claim. Several paragraphs later, it is revealed that this consultant's company was being sued in Nevada for fraudulent signature collection.

Reporters and politicos may believe these claims because unlike advertising or candidate appearances, much of the work of voter contact takes place out of the public eye: within offices, at the doors, over the phones, and increasingly through text and email. Given the resources that recent campaigns devoted to field organization and their public-facing rhetoric about the importance of knocking doors, there is a clear belief among campaigns that setting up a field office can help them win votes but little verification of this assumption.

Like many campaign activities, measuring effects is tricky. As detailed in previous work and the preceding Section, campaigns do not place field offices randomly, making causal inference difficult. Campaign effects are likely to be subtle, given the overwhelming influence of partisan identity on vote choice, and isolating one tactic from the array of strategies used by campaigns is a challenge. Previous work on the subject has used data from single elections (Masket 2009; Masket et al. 2016; Weinschenk 2015) and across multiple cycles (Darr and Levendusky 2014) to measure the impact of field offices on votes.

In this section, we update this literature to include more recent data allowing us to discern differences between Democratic and Republican campaigns. Given the consistent use of field offices by Republicans across the 2012, 2016, and 2020 elections, we can make inferences about the relative effectiveness of Democratic and Republican offices. We also examine potential moderators of field office effectiveness, including factors determining placement such as rurality and political competitiveness. Finally, we use data from the Cooperative Election Study (CES) in 2012, 2016, and 2020 to show how field office presence in a county influences respondents' likelihood of being contacted by a campaign in-person, over the phone, by email or text, or through the mail (Darr and Levendusky 2014; Masket et al. 2016).

By updating these analyses to reflect recent trends toward waning Democratic field investment and resurgent Republican interest in the field, we can learn more about where and how these offices can give campaigns better returns on their investments. The value of campaign offices for staffers and volunteers is apparent in interviews but difficult to quantify, and the willingness of campaign leadership to continue funding these operations may depend upon their belief that opening offices leads to better performance in the places that matter.

4.1 Why Storefronts Should Work

The emergence of field experimentation in political science preceded the resurgence of field operations in campaigns by a few years. As we discuss in Section 2, starting in the late 1990s and into early 2000s, scholars at the Institute for Social and Policy Studies (ISPS) at Yale University began conducting field experiments about the relative effectiveness of various tactics for increasing civic participation. The literature they produced is broad and influential, but two findings stand out for our purposes: that knocking on doors raises turnout by roughly 10 percentage points (Gerber and Green 2000), and that the most effective means for increasing turnout is social pressure involving one's neighbors (Gerber et al. 2008). Field offices provide campaigns an easy way to generate the raw materials of in-person interaction, local volunteers, and volunteer training that should lead to effective voter mobilization.

The strategic behavior of campaigns makes it difficult to consistently identify the effects of a field office. The strategies of Republicans and Democrats are not random and thus any attempt to discover their effects must account as thoroughly as possible for unobserved and observed variation between counties to minimize the biases from strategic placement.

Keeping these inferential limitations in mind, previous studies have nonetheless found evidence of field effects across a variety of elections and models. The first study of field offices, by Seth Masket in *Public Opinion Quarterly* (2009), modeled the results of the 2008 election in terms of changes in vote share and office placement from 2004 and competition between the Obama and McCain campaigns. Masket identifies a 0.8 percent increase in Democratic vote share in the counties where Obama opened a field office, and that Obama's offices performed particularly well in areas where Kerry had not opened an office.

Masket revisited these models for the 2012 election with coauthors Lynn Vavreck and John Sides (2016), finding somewhat smaller effects: a 0.29 percent increase for Obama in counties without a Romney office, and that generally Obama's offices were more strongly associated with increased Democratic vote share than Romney's offices were with Republican vote share. Finally, modeling only turnout using a lagged dependent variable model, Aaron Weinschenk (2015) found a small positive effect on turnout for Obama and Romney offices, with a significant effect only for Obama's when modeled alongside Romney's (Weinschenk 2015, Table 3, column d).

These single-election snapshots take care to control for the most consequential covariates, such as county-level measurements of race, age, income, and vote share in the previous presidential election to capture county-level aggregate partisanship and reveal some general trend: field offices have small but measurable effects, and Democratic offices appear to be more impactful than their Republican counterparts. Darr (2020) updated these models to include 2016, continuing to find an association between Democratic office placement and vote share: a 0.99 percent increase in the Masket, Sides and Vavreck models for areas with a Clinton office only, and a 0.81 percent increase for each Clinton office located in a county. These findings are complicated somewhat by the overall decrease in offices by both the Clinton and Trump campaigns, compared to their predecessors in 2012, but overall show a continued small benefit for Democrats and negligible returns for Republicans.

4.2 Impact across Elections

Darr and Levendusky (2014) present the only estimate of field office effects across multiple elections (2004, 2008, and 2012), using repeated observations of counties in a fixed-effects regression model. Their model, represented mathematically in Model 1, accounts for unobserved heterogeneity between counties, states, and years. These county, state, and year fixed effects account for changes in what might otherwise be included as covariates at those levels, such as population, partisanship, or income. As the authors note, however, these analyses require updating in future research: only Democrats are measured, and the 2004 and 2008 elections did not include substantial Republican efforts. In this section, we update these analyses to include results from the 2012, 2016, and 2020 elections for Republicans.

We adopt the same models and general approach of Darr and Levendusky (2014), including a model measuring only whether there is an office from the specified party's nominee in that county; a model measuring whether those offices are more effective in battleground states; and a model assessing if offices are more or less impactful in counties with larger or smaller populations. These analyses are each based on the same model, represented in Equation 1.

$$yit = \beta 0 + \beta 1 FOit + \Gamma Zit + \alpha i + \delta s(i),t + \varepsilon it \tag{1}$$

In this model, yit is (a) turnout in county i in election t, or (b) Democratic presidential vote share in county i at election t, FOit is in an indicator for whether county i has one or more Democratic or Republican field office(s) at election t, Zit represents county-level control variables, αi is a set of county-level fixed effects, $\delta s(i),t$ is a set of state-year fixed effects, and ε is an error term (Darr and Levendusky 2014).

For these analyses, we wanted to capture each party's field offices over three elections, as Darr and Levendusky did. This meant using different elections for each party, however: we used 2008, 2012, and 2016, the peak years for Democratic candidates, and 2012, 2016, and 2020 for Republicans. While it would be ideal to compare across the same elections, the special circumstances of covid-19 and Democratic avoidance of field in 2020 make that difficult. Given that these models do not include competition, each should give a good sense of the effectiveness of each party's offices across multiple elections and contribute to our knowledge of whether storefront campaigning is similarly effective for both parties.

Table 1 gives the results for partisan vote share across these elections. Columns 1–3 replicate Darr and Levendusky (2014) for Democrats and find some key differences from those conclusions based on 2004, 2008, and 2012. First, merely having a field office in a county in any state (Column 1) is not

Table 1 Partisan vote share by Democratic (2008, 2012, 2016) and Republican (2012, 2016, 2020) field office by county

	(1)	(2)	(3)	(4)	(5)	(6)
	Democrats Democratic vote %			Republicans Republican vote %		
Field office in county	−0.318	−0.775*	−0.348*	0.851*	1.297*	0.964*
	(0.163)	(0.271)	(0.159)	(0.298)	(0.640)	(0.296)
Battleground state		10.634*			−0.506*	
		(0.632)			(0.175)	
Office X battleground		0.714*			−0.580	
		(0.328)			(0.697)	
Office X county pop.			0.312			−0.616
			(0.610)			(0.484)
Constant	31.611*	28.866*	31.567*	64.827*	65.011*	64.864*
	(0.048)	(0.169)	(0.051)	(0.049)	(0.087)	(0.049)
Observations	9,335	9,335	9,329	9,335	9,335	9,330
R-squared	0.849	0.849	0.849	0.584	0.584	0.584
Number of counties	3,112	3,112	3,110	3,112	3,112	3,110

Note. Robust standard errors in parentheses. * $p < 0.05$.

positively or significantly associated with increases in Democratic vote share. Within battleground states, having a Democratic office led to 0.714 percent higher Democratic vote share compared to battleground state areas without an office. Democratic offices seem more potent in the states that mattered most, and while we cannot rule out the deepening urban/rural divide as either cause or consequence of these actions, our within-county state-year fixed effects approach gives us confidence in the validity of these results.

Columns 4–6 represent the first published analysis of Republican office effects across multiple elections, and present a very different story than analyses based solely on Democrats. In a reversal of the findings in Columns 1–3, Republican offices had a positive influence on Republican vote share (0.85 percent; Column 4). However, this positive effect comes with an important qualification: within battleground states, where additional votes are most needed, the coefficient was negative and indistinguishable from zero (Column 5). Republican offices, overall, seem to be roughly where Democratic offices were after Darr and Levendusky's assessment (2014), but without positive coefficients on the two models with interactions: battleground states and high-population counties. The intercept term also warrants discussion: since most counties in America are rural, analyses of Republican vote share start at a much higher level (roughly 64 percent) than the analyses of Democratic vote share in Columns 1–3 (roughly 30 percent).

Taken together, these findings show that Republicans may benefit from field offices broadly, but not specifically in higher-population areas or in battleground states, where the most strategically important votes are located. It should also be noted that these results do not match Darr and Levendusky's findings, reflecting changes in politics over the intervening years: Republicans gained strength in rural counties while Democrats solidified their strength in more populated urban areas and attracted more suburban votes during the Trump elections. Field offices continue to be correlated with higher partisan vote share, but as politics changes, the strategies of the two parties remain flexible.

Next, we turn to the question of turnout: do field offices increase political participation broadly? This outcome variable is likely not an explicit goal of campaigns when opening these offices: campaigns care much more about differential partisan turnout being in their favor than they do higher turnout for the sake of democratic participation. However, it stands to reason that areas with campaign field offices would increase turnout for the campaign in the area (Darr and Levendusky 2014; Weinschenk 2015), and possibly for the opposition as well if there is backlash (Bailey et al. 2016; Heersink et al. 2021).

Table 2 gives the results for turnout in areas with and without field offices across the relevant elections. Once again, the results diverge from Darr and

Table 2 Turnout by Democratic (2008, 2012, 2016) and Republican (2012, 2016, 2020) field office by county

	(1)	(2)	(3)	(4)	(5)	(6)
	Democrats Turnout			**Republicans Turnout**		
Field office in county	−0.147	−0.102	−0.181	0.309*	0.231	0.286*
	(0.099)	(0.148)	(0.104)	(0.124)	(0.252)	(0.125)
Battleground state		4.014*			−4.998*	
		(0.544)			(0.201)	
Office X battleground		−0.064			0.102	
		(0.186)			(0.265)	
Office X county pop.			0.402*			0.131
			(0.150)			(0.083)
Constant	44.685*	43.655*	44.683*	49.557*	51.353*	49.558*
	(0.029)	(0.143)	(0.035)	(0.032)	(0.085)	(0.032)
Observations	9,331	9,332	9,329	9,331	9,331	9,330
R-squared	0.375	0.290	0.290	0.790	0.790	0.790
Number of counties	3,112	3,112	3,110	3,111	3,111	3,110

Note. Robust standard errors in parentheses. * $p < 0.05$.

Levendusky (2014): having a Democratic office in a county did not translate into higher turnout except in higher population counties (0.402 percent; Column 3). These counties tend to be more Democratic, and so this result should encourage Democrats to pursue strategies that require field offices. Republican offices are positively correlated with turnout overall (0.309 percent; Column 4) and in less-populated counties (0.286 percent; Column 6), which, again, is a likely Republican goal given their performance there in recent elections. The intercept terms are far more equal, with a slightly higher starting point in the models of Republican offices (50 percent vs. 44 percent).

These updates of the findings in Darr and Levendusky (2014) add to our understanding of field office effectiveness and provide higher confidence in causal validity than single-election snapshots, though no observational approach is perfect. There is a clear partisan difference in areas of higher population and those with more political competition: within battleground states and in more populous areas, Democrats reap more benefits from opening a field office.

Nationwide and in less-populated counties, however, Republicans see greater effects from their offices. The good news for Republicans is that there are many, many more counties that are small, rural, and Republican than there are populous cities in battleground states. The bad news is that battleground states decide the winner, and there is no extra credit for winning more counties. Both Republicans and Democrats may interpret these results as encouraging a storefront-based strategy: as noted throughout Section 3, however, the success of that strategy depends in large part on where those offices are located and whether there are enough voters to make a difference.

4.3 Adjusting the Game Plan: Changes between Elections

Single-election snapshots lack the causal mechanisms needed to show that field offices are impacting vote share in a positive or negative way. They can tell us something about the areas of opportunity and consequences of strategies, however, and help us to understand how campaigns learned from their prede-cessors. Given the still-evolving status of in-person mobilization in the age of digital and data-driven campaigning, these cycle-to-cycle dynamics are crucial for determining where field offices fit into campaigns' strategies and cultures following wins and losses (Kreiss 2016). To learn how campaigns learn, we base our analyses on models of field office effects as a function of previous office placement, using the specification from Seth Masket's examination of the 2008 campaign (Masket 2009).

Several factors from 2004 and 2008 make Masket's models ripe for updating. McCain's field effort was substantially weaker than Obama's, and the data on his office locations is unreliable (see Darr and Levendusky 2014); similarly, in 2004, John Kerry's field effort was supplemented by offices opened by an outside group called "America Coming Together." As such, the 2004 to 2008 period – though marked by the Obama campaign's historic and still unsurpassed investment in the field – represented something of a transition for the practice of field organizing. Subsequent campaigns settled into more of a standard approach: coordinated with state and local parties but led by the campaign, with several hundred offices opened in battleground states.

The model used by Masket (2009) estimates a change in the partisan vote share (Democrats only, in his case) and an interaction of field office presence in 2004 and 2008, each represented by a dummy variable: 1 if the county hosted an office, and 0 if it did not. He also included a host of control variables: change in unemployment, population growth, race, age, income, population, and county-level partisan vote share in the previous election. Ours is similar, with the exception of change in unemployment captured as change from the previous year, rather than July to October of the election year. Though this analysis is subject to some of the concerns about causality described earlier in this Section, these covariates (particularly lagged partisan vote share) are helpful. Results for the interaction terms are shown as coefficient plots in Figure 13, with full regression results in Table A4.1 of the Online Appendix. We also follow Masket's model by restricting our sample to battleground states only.

Democratic campaigns since 2008 are living in the shadow of the 2008 Obama campaign's massive investment in the field that saw nearly 1,000 offices opened across the country. Obama's 2012 operation, therefore, had fewer places to open offices that were not there before. In the analyses of the Obama 2012 campaign in Figure 13, none of the coefficients are distinguishable from zero. The campaign may have lost a bit of ground in areas where they did not follow in the 2008 campaign's footsteps and may have improved slightly in the areas where they both opened offices, but neither rises to the level of statistical significance.

Clinton's campaign, curiously, did significantly better in one category: areas where Obama opened an office in 2012 but Clinton campaign did not in 2016. Since Obama 2012 opened roughly 200 more offices than Clinton, this is not a small subsample. Clinton may have left some favorable counties unorganized in 2016, though it is not possible in this analysis to say if adding field offices would have increased that advantage.

The results for Republicans in 2016 and 2020, the cycles for which there is reliable data for the preceding election, call into question the targeting strategies of the Trump campaign, particularly in 2020. The results show that Trump lost ground in areas where he opened a 2020 office but not 2016, and again, this was not a small category since he opened more than 100 additional offices in 2020

Change in partisan vote share from previous election

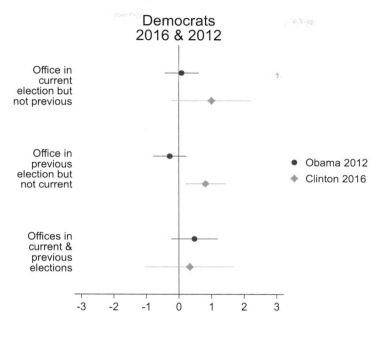

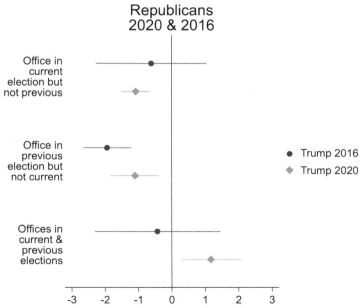

Figure 13 Change in vote share and office placement across elections, 2012, 2016, and 2020. Models replicate those from Masket (2009). Full results in Table A4.1 of the Online Appendix

than 2016. In both elections, Trump's campaign did worse in areas where only the preceding campaign opened offices.

While the strategic merits of "offense" or "defense" are up for debate, Trump did worse in areas he ignored across both cycles. It is possible, however, that his 2020 operation was more effective following his more serious commitment to the effort and science of ground operations. In areas with offices in both 2016 and 2020, the relationship with Republican vote share is significant and positive.

Over the past decade of field organizing, Democratic and Republican presidential campaigns did not simply copy their predecessors. These offices are not closed and reopened across cycles. There are clear, election-specific decisions made about how to spend limited resources, and where it might be most valuable for increasing vote share and vote totals in the places where it will matter most for receiving 270 electoral votes (Shaw 2006). The gradual decline in Democratic office locations makes it somewhat difficult to determine whether offices are more effective at increasing vote share, though most coefficients in the analyses are weakly positive and not distinguishable from zero. The variation in Republican offices, with peaks for Romney 2012 and Trump 2020, tells a somewhat clearer story about where offices might work. Should subsequent GOP nominees match or expand upon Trump's sizable 2020 operation, we should be able to learn more about how past strategies can inform effectiveness.

4.4 Home Field and Away Games

Are these trends merely a function of history, however, or are they better explained by the competitiveness of counties? Past patterns are based somewhat on election-specific factors such as campaigns' perceptions of swing and core counties, as described in Section 3. Are offices more effective in core counties, where campaigns can "run up the score," or in swing counties, where voters might be more malleable and open to in-person appeals?

The analyses in Section 3 showed that Republicans are more likely to invest in swing counties than are Democrats, who prefer to maximize their votes from their more populous core counties. By modeling the interaction of office placement with county competitiveness, we may be able to determine whether these differences in strategies work for their respective parties.

In the models below, we substitute vote share percentage in the given election for change between elections. We use the same county-level covariates as described above in the Masket (2009) replication models: change in population and unemployment, total population, race, education, income, and lagged partisan vote share, with analyses limited to battleground states. We add an interaction term for office placement (0 if no office, 1 if any office) and a three-category competitiveness variable: opponent, swing, and core. Each of these models is calculated and run separately by party and election, and competitiveness is redefined for each party and year. Results are presented in the same figure for ease of comparison and interpretation in Figure 14.

Overall, county competitiveness is not a substantial influence on office effectiveness for either party. Among Democrats, the Obama and Clinton campaigns did not have consistent trends. Obama fared a bit worse in 2012 when his campaign did not open an office in swing counties, and interestingly, Clinton seems to have fared better in core counties without an office in 2016. As in the previous analyses with prior offices, it is unclear if Clinton missed an opportunity in these counties or perhaps fared better because she avoided a backlash (Bailey et al. 2016).

For Republicans, there are similarly few significant effects. The lone exceptions are with Trump 2016, where he performed better in both swing and core counties without an office. Given the low number of offices opened by his campaign, and Trump's substantial margins of victory in small, rural counties in 2016, this is an unsurprising finding. None of the coefficients for Romney in 2012 or Trump's unopposed 2020 effort are significantly different from zero.

Core, swing, and opponent counties do not show much evidence of differential field office effects. This should cast a differently light upon the finding that Republicans target swing and Democrats target core counties. Republican core counties in these analyses are by and large rural counties with low populations and a high degree of difficulty for canvassers. Democratic core counties, on the other hand, are more likely to be urban with higher populations. Even small effects may increase overall votes enough to tip a battleground state's outcome, as Obama's offices likely did in North Carolina in 2008 (Darr and Levendusky 2014).

Republicans' calculus is different because their core counties are more difficult to organize. Since there seems to be no added benefit to investing in swing counties, their primary strategic difference from Democrats, it seems Republicans do not benefit as much from offices.

4.5 Farm Teams and the Big City

Whether a county is urban or rural matters for Democratic and Republican investment strategies, as seen in Section 3. But do the parties' offices perform differently according to these county characteristics? Organizing may be more difficult in spacious rural areas, but if Republican office openings are rewarded with even higher performance, it may be worth a broader strategy with more offices in more rural counties. Similarly, if Democrats benefit only in urban

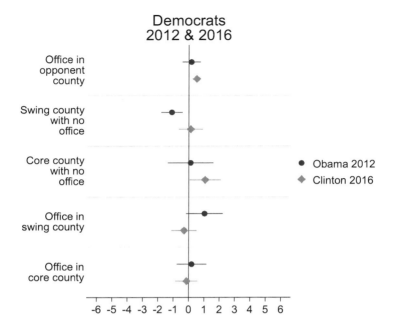

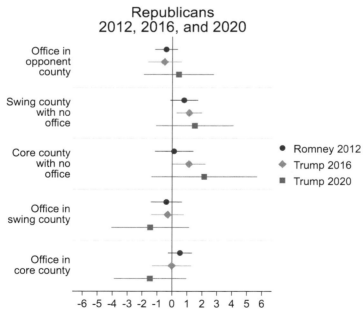

Figure 14 Influence of Democratic and Republican field offices on partisan vote share by swing and core counties, 2012, 2016, and 2020. Full results in Table A4.2 of the Online Appendix

areas, it would incentivize saturating the cities in battleground states to maximize their statewide totals.

We test this possibility using the same model as our tests of county competitiveness, but replace that three-category variable with a recoding of the nine-category urban-rural continuum codes compiled by the Economic Research Service of the Department of Agriculture, recoded to urban (1–3), suburban (4–6), and rural (7–9). We once again restrict our sample to the battleground states in each election. The results are presented as marginal predicted probabilities in Figure 15, with full regression results in Table A4.3 of the online appendix.

The differences between the parties are once again clear: Democrats generally benefit from having a field office in a county, while Republican counties with field offices fare slightly worse than similar counties without one. Democrats seem to benefit the least from suburban offices, since the increase between estimates of areas with and without offices is lowest in those cases. Obama's 2012 campaign seems to have added more with an office in rural areas than urban areas, but again, these analyses do not take into account the value gained by organizing high-population counties. Clinton sees no such advantage of organizing rural areas, and the differences between urban and rural counties are much larger.

Most results on the Republican side show the exact opposite: lower predicted performance in areas with field offices across the urban, rural, and suburban categories. The notable exception is Romney in 2012, who seems to have benefited greatly from organizing in rural areas but not urban or suburban counties. This result is a clear outlier, but it is possible that Romney's success organizing rural areas could have been a harbinger of Trump's unexpected and massive overperformance in rural areas in 2016. These rural areas were ready to support Republican candidates, and Trump appealed to them even if his 2016 field operations were too small to reach them.

The most important takeaway from these analyses is that, generally, Democrats are expected to do better in areas with field offices and Republicans are expected to do worse, across each of the elections and candidates observed. Democrats appear to have a home field advantage when it comes to field offices. It is unclear why Republican offices are ineffective – contacting fewer voters, or generating higher backlash, perhaps – but regardless, the GOP nominees do not seem to be benefiting from offices in the states where they should matter most.

4.6 Blocking and Tackling: Evidence of Voter Contact

We have discussed placement strategy and office effectiveness in detail, but so far have not presented evidence supporting the assertion that campaigns use these offices to contact voters. This is, of course, the point of field offices: placing staff

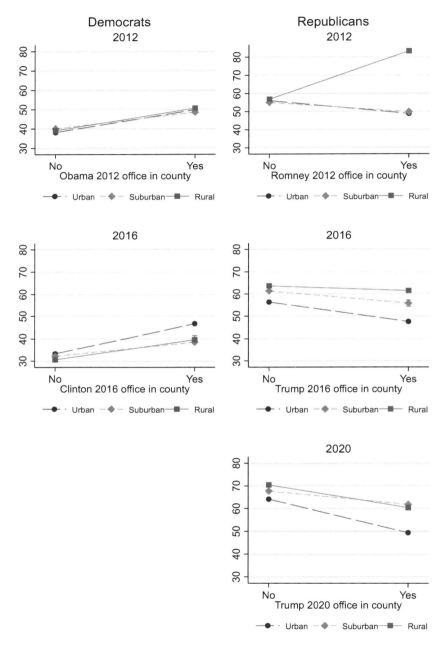

Figure 15 Marginal predicted probabilities of field office effectiveness by county rurality, measured as urban, suburban, or rural, 2012, 2016, and 2020. Full results in Table A4.3 of the Online Appendix

resources closer to groups of critical voters, training volunteers to contact those voters directly, and creating a positive data feedback loop to assist with targeting. If areas with field offices do not experience higher levels of voter contact, that may be evidence that field offices were ineffective or poorly used.

Did voters in areas with field offices report more contact from campaigns, and in particular the types of contact – in-person and phone – most associated with a local office? We replicated logit models from Masket et al. (2016) using survey data from the 2020 Cooperative Congressional Election Study (Schaffner et al. 2021), and will also compare results to the replication of these models in the 2012 and 2016 election (Ansolabehere et al. 2017; Darr 2020; Masket et al. 2016). As before, the main difference of 2020 from prior elections is that there are no interactions for competition since Biden did not have offices.

Individual-level covariates included battleground state residency; voter registration status; voting in the previous election; age (in years); and dummy variables for gender (female), race and ethnicity (Black, Hispanic, Asian, other), union member (current and former), self or family in military, home ownership, born-again evangelical, education, income, and marital status. The types of contact measured are: any contact, which is a summary of the specific measures; in-person contact; phone contact; email contact; or receiving mail from the campaign. Results are presented in Figures 16 and 17 as marginal

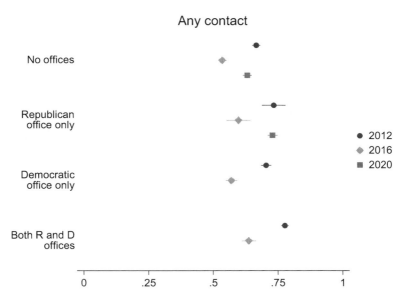

Figure 16 Estimates of any contact by campaigns, 2012, 2016, and 2020. Data from CCES. Full results in Table A4.4a of the Online Appendix

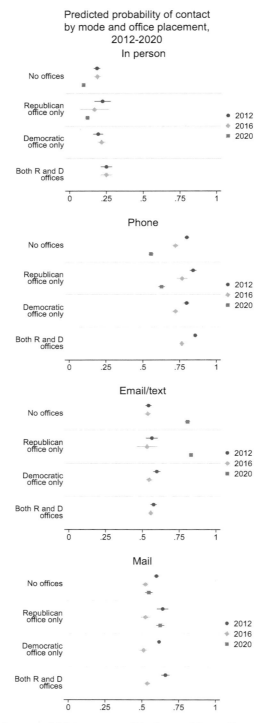

Figure 17 Estimates of (a) in-person, (b) phone, (c) email or text, or (d) mail contact from campaigns, 2012, 2016, and 2020. Data from CCES. Full results in Table A4.4b, c, d, and e of the Online Appendix

predicted probabilities, and in Online Appendix Table A4.4a, b, c, d, and e with the logit coefficients translated to odds ratios for ease of interpretation.

Respondents in counties with offices consistently report more contact of all kinds across the years measured, as displayed in Figure 16. The highest amount of predicted contact is in areas of highest competition, counties with both campaigns' offices, in 2012, the year of our sample with the most total campaign offices. In 2016, voter contact is consistently lower across both parties and competitive and uncompetitive areas alike, supporting other evidence that field operations were simply not as robust in that election cycle. Self-reported contact in 2020 more closely resembles 2012 than 2016, possibly showing a bounce back for voter contact operations after their dip in the 2016 cycle – particularly given that only one campaign was in the field during the 2020 cycle.

Not every form of voter contact is enhanced by field offices, however. There is no theoretical reason to believe that mail or email contact should increase if a campaign opens a storefront in a neighborhood. Phone calls are a major function of field offices, but many campaigns also now have call tools that allow volunteers to call voters from their own homes. The type of contact that should be most responsive to field office presence is in-person contact: by placing volunteers close to voters' homes, providing walk lists of houses to visit, and training volunteers to have productive, face-to-face conversations, field offices give campaigns the opportunity to coordinate and provide the materials necessary for in-person contact. Figure 17 shows predicted probabilities of each mode of contact by year, using the model above (Masket et al. 2016).

In-person is the least common form of contact by campaigns, with only 25 percent or fewer voters predicted to be contacted in-person in any given cycle. In 2020, due to the covid-19 pandemic, lack of competition, or both, there is less than half of the contact predicted in areas with no offices as in 2012 or 2016. Though areas with a Republican office only show a slight increase in in-person contact, the rates of contact remain lower than other cycles – particularly 2012. As expected, in high-competition areas (those with both parties' offices in 2012 and 2016), in-person contact rates are the highest.

While phone calls are more widely deployed than in-person contact, there is a clear decline in the use of this tactic by campaigns from 2012 to 2020. Regardless of the presence or absence of offices, phone contact fell by roughly 20 percent over this period. Areas with offices are predicted to report more phone calls in general, and once again areas with both offices have the highest rates of contact. This linear decrease in phone contact shows a strategic shift by campaigns, for whom phone banking is usually emphasized and valued as a tactic (Gerber and Green 2000; Nickerson 2006). Whatever the reason, the sharp decrease of phone contact is worth watching in future cycles.

The most apparent outlier across any of these forms of voter contact is email and/or text contact in 2020, which jumps significantly relative to previous years. In areas with and without offices, roughly 80 percent of people are predicted to be contacted by email or text, compared to around 55 percent in previous cycles. Services like ThruText made "text banking" a low-risk volunteer activity with a smaller time commitment and less social awkwardness than phone banking or knocking doors (senior Democrat, personal communication, September 1, 2022).

This is perhaps the central question going forward for future elections: will the rates of text and email contact remain at 2020's elevated levels at the expense of more personal forms of contact? If campaigns feel that texting is effective and personal, it should reduce the need for field offices: text trainings can be done over Zoom, and the available tools make the process of contact extremely efficient.

Texting undoubtedly allows campaigns to reach more voters in a cost-effective manner (Fowler and Ridout 2013; Stromer-Galley 2014). In keeping with the "relational organizing" that defined Obama's NTL model, personable friend-to-friend texting can significantly increase turnout (see Schein et al. 2021). Texting may be particularly useful as a reminder to vote once registered, serving as a "noticeable reminder" that reduces the costs of voting (Dale and Strauss 2009). In recent years, however, the evidence is more mixed. Meta-analyses over a longer time frame consistently show inconsequential turnout effects of impersonal contact such as texts (Green and Gerber 2019). Yan and Bernhard (2024) show evidence of a gendered backlash effect whereby female volunteers who send a political text were more likely to be silenced and receive hostile replies than their male counterparts. Texts are poorly regulated, take place out of the public eye, and often spread divisive and deceptive content, which could turn voters off and decrease the effectiveness of legitimate campaign messages (Singer 2022). Many of the studies showing that texting is effective came from before it was a ubiquitous practice (Malhotra et al. 2011): In the lead-up to election day in 2020, an excess of 80 million political text messages were sent daily (Bajak and Burke 2020), raising the possibility of backlash.

Covid-19 cut down on the more personal forms of campaign communication, though Trump's offices did have a clear correlation with in-person and phone call voter contact. The technological infrastructure for digital, text-based campaigning is now in place. Upcoming contests will show whether phone contact rates continue to drop and if text contact levels return to historically normal rates.

4.7 Three Yards and a Cloud of Dust

Most campaign tactics are not supported by rigorous empirical evidence of their effectiveness (Issenberg 2012). The largest expenditure for campaigns, by far, is advertising on television. Presidential elections are essentially subsidies to local television stations in swing states, with hundreds of millions of dollars going to reach voters in their living rooms. Political scientists who study this tactic, however, are less bullish than the consultants who write the ads and buy the airtime. The most thorough study conducted on television ads, published in the journal *Science*, summarizes what we know about ads with a title worth stating in full: "The small effects of political advertising are small regardless of context, message, sender, or receiver: Evidence from 59 real-time randomized experiments" (Coppock et al. 2020). Even the most expensive, widely used campaigning tactic is dubiously effective, across many possible attributes of the message, time frames, and audiences.

It would therefore be surprising if we found slam-dunk evidence of substantial field office effects, particularly given that their locations cannot be randomized without unprecedented candidate buy-in (Issenberg 2012). In this section, we presented evidence from across elections and from individual campaigns in 2012, 2016, and 2020 that generally supports the idea that field offices can move votes in the campaign's desired direction, but in different contexts by political party. Democrats seem to have the advantage in battleground states, while Republicans may be benefiting from an expanded footprint but face a geographically diffuse base that is difficult to contact at their doors or gather in a central location. In either case, any effects are small: the campaign ground game resembles former Ohio State football coach Woody Hayes' famously methodical and unexciting rushing offense, known as "three yards and a cloud of dust."

Previous studies found that field offices were most effective for Democrats and with unclear results for Republicans. Ours is the first study to assess both parties over multiple elections, while adding the context of moderators such as county competitiveness and rurality in individual cycles. In general, our findings confirm that Democrats may have a built-in advantage in many cases when it comes to storefront-based organizing. Republicans can benefit as well, but would likely need a much larger investment in rural areas to maximize base turnout (Panagopoulos 2020). Given the rise in convenience voting practices in 2020 and the suspicion with which many Republicans (from Trump down) view those expansions, in-person organizing might be particularly beneficial for explaining the value of early and absentee voting to Republican voters.

All studies of presidential elections suffer from the same issue: a small sample size. The study of campaign storefronts is no exception. There has been substantial variation in campaigns' commitment to the tactic over the past two decades, including an aberration in 2020 that may push the practice of voter outreach down a different, digitized path. While field experiments show that in-person contact and social situations are the most effective means to get voters to the polls, the infrastructure required to implement them by campaigns can be expensive and time consuming compared to off-the-shelf digital solutions.

5 The Future of Field

The metaphor of field offices remained strong on the Democratic side in 2020, even though there were no physical offices to be found. The internet became a "battleground state" in its own right, as Biden organizers sought out potential supporters in Facebook groups and on Twitter based on their posts and group memberships (Alter 2020). Initial contacts over text messages were the "front door" of the campaign. Slack channels were the "office" where people could chat and socialize. Instead of building their team by working shoulder-to-shoulder, campaign organizers who have never met "become a close-knit team through daily Google Hangouts and FaceTime calls" (Alter 2020). Official Democratic party Facebook groups transformed into "virtual field offices," in the campaign's words:

> These offices are run by paid organizers, who ensure members show up to digital events and spread Biden's message on their respective networks. The goal is to replicate the same level of "relational organizing that you'd get in a field office" ... invoking Obama's 2008 strategy, which relied on people recruiting their friends and family. (Alter 2020)

Biden's success without offices in 2020 raises the question of whether campaigns will consider storefronts to be worth the investment in future cycles. These descriptions of the Biden digital operation show the immense impact of the field offices-driven model from Obama and Clinton: organizers and volunteers repeatedly reach for similarities with physical offices while discussing their digital strategies.

As Michael Bloomberg's ill-fated 2020 primary campaign showed, however, the office itself does not vote, volunteer, or train: you need committed organizers conducting effective community outreach to potential volunteers that become effective canvassers and callers, not just four walls and some passed hors d'oeuvres (Ruiz 2020a). Offices provide the place where these things can happen effectively, but campaigns must be sufficiently organized and inspirational to take advantage of those benefits.

Biden built an impressive operation during the campaign, but digital tools for modeling preferences and assisting with voter contact tends to proliferate even more following a campaign once campaign leadership takes that expertise into private industry (Kreiss 2016). These tools are then made available to future campaigns through these business and shape methods of voter contact. For instance, Democrats' technological superiority through 2012 was shaped by Dean's successes and failures in 2004, Obama's investment in tech and triumph in 2008, and the surrounding technological infrastructure that emerged (Kreiss 2016).

A senior Democrat explained to us how technological tools determined what was possible. In 2020, the event-planning digital tool MobilizeAmerica became a "steady home" for volunteers "to find out what you can do locally." Biden's team used "a very, very simple dialer tool that in every way made it like a coloring book in a kindergarten classroom ... We have to build something that is so simple that any volunteer from any campaign can utilize to get over the learning curve, and won't have to do a whole host of training."

For a sense of community, "Slack was certainly, certainly something we couldn't have lived without" (senior Democrat, personal communication, September 1, 2022). Republicans lack data and technological infrastructure on the level of Democrats, for reasons detailed by Kreiss (2016), but made a much more serious investment in recruiting and training office-based field organizers in 2020 that could put them in a stronger position in future election cycles.

In this Element, we used twenty years of original data on field office locations to explain why they should be effective; discern the considerations for office placement; measure the effects of opening an office; and assess differences between the parties. Using original maps within states and metropolitan areas, we tracked a clear decline in Democratic offices that still exceeded Republican investment in the field until 2020, when those dynamics were flipped by covid-19. Within metropolitan areas, the Obama 2012 campaign saturated inner cities and suburbs while Clinton's lighter touch may have cost her crucial votes. Republicans, in general, were likelier to contest swing counties while Democrats focused on areas of core support to increase their numbers in areas of strength.

We discovered a "home field advantage" for Democrats, who can open many offices in their densely packed urban and suburban base areas within battleground states while Republicans face a geographically diffuse base of support that is difficult to organize in-person. Democratic offices continue to have a positive influence on Democratic vote share in battleground states, while Republican offices do not.

There are not substantial differences in field office effectiveness across urban, rural, or suburban areas, or swing and core areas. Democratic performance is steadier than Republicans, who seem to fare poorly in areas where their partisan predecessors invested but they ignored. In general, our models showed that Democrats fared better in areas where they opened an office, but Republicans were less helped by setting up a storefront. Since Republicans were the only party that opened offices in the most recent cycle, 2020, the future of field offices remains in doubt. We also found evidence that e-mail and/or text contact skyrocketed in 2020, as we would expect during the pandemic.

Future investments in the field may be directed toward areas of strength and need in an evolving political climate. Densely populated and transient communities like East Las Vegas should remain targets for Democrats, while suburban offices could help Republicans staunch the bleeding in the suburbs and reach their rural support base. This strategy may represent a more efficient use of resources for the GOP than opening offices in urban neighborhoods. Reporting suggests Republicans are in fact turning away from these types of offices, despite the rhetoric from our interviewees: all ten remaining community centers were closed in March 2024 (King and Bender 2024).

Based on our findings and interviews, it seems likely that office-based and digital methods of recruiting and deploying volunteers and contacting voters will have to exist side-by-side in the future, and it is not clear how (or if) that will work. Campaigns seem interested in field options that are not candidate-controlled, working with outside groups to outsource those activities. While our interviews make it clear that campaigns prefer to have offices for staff morale and volunteer recruitment, time will tell who will conduct that work and how it will collaborate or compete with technology-focused methods of voter contact.

5.1 The Case for Distributed Organizing

Though this Element is primarily about the value of renting physical space and establishing a storefront office, there are genuine benefits to a distributed, digitized approach that diverges further from the candidate-centered organizing that defined presidential campaign organizing in recent cycles. These options are worth considering as we try to project into future election cycles. Previous research and our interviews with former campaign organizers provide several reasons why campaigns might prefer to keep voter contact online.

First, digital tools have developed to the point where they are easy to use by volunteers and campaign staff (Kreiss 2016). Tools like ThruTalk and ThruText, used by Democrats in 2020, do the dialing for volunteers and speeds through the more tedious aspects of phone or text banking. Texting also allows campaigns more control over what their volunteers say to voters: from the initial message to suggested follow-ups and scripts for individual issues, texting allows volunteers the time to gather themselves and consult campaign resources before they reply.

These tools can mitigate the principal-agent issue directly by standardizing the message, but also arguably takes the personal touch out of these interactions.

Scale and access are also a major consideration. It is much easier to contact greater numbers of voters digitally, thanks to calling and texting tools that message broadly and make calls automatically until someone picks up. Moreover, these actions can be taken by anyone anywhere, not just those living in the most competitive areas of the most competitive states. There are rarely more than ten battleground states in a given election, and plenty of counties within those states do not have field offices. Those without transportation to the office or with physical disabilities are also disadvantaged by an emphasis on gathering in-person. By bringing more people in digitally, campaigns sacrifice the demonstrated effectiveness of local volunteers but maximize the number of voters they can reach and volunteers they can engage. Campaigns may choose quantity over quality if the increase in quantity is deemed more consequential than the decrease in contact quality.

Campaigns may also genuinely prefer a group-based distributed approach, where members of "coalitions" contact one another, to a geography-based voter contact system. The mechanism behind the effectiveness of local-to-local contact is that those voters share something important in common (Sinclair et al. 2013). Group-based organizing, connecting (for example) African-American voters to each other, environmentalists to environmentalists, the religious to the religious, and so forth, should work the same way, without the constraints of geography. In our discussions with a senior Democrat, he commented that the ability to "meet people where they are" with regard to local vs. coalition-based organizing was a major advantage of the distributed approach.

> Local to local was still the ideal, but this is one thing that actually the distributed and digital approach allowed us to do a lot easier than in past campaigns when you don't have to lean as heavily into that – is truly to meet people where they are ... There is tension on the ground, that one person came in through their neighborhood team, but another came in via, let's say for example, through a coalition group like African-Americans for Biden: they live in this area but they don't want to organize with their neighborhood folks, they want to organize with African-Americans for Biden. There was always that tension. The distributed approach allowed us to not have that tension and meet people where they are. (senior Democrat, personal communication, September 1, 2022)

Since group membership is increasingly linked to partisanship – a powerful identity of its own, if not the most powerful for politics – speaking to people within their identity groups might be an effective method of organizing (Achen and Bartels 2016; Mason 2018). Whether those identities are racial and ethnic, veterans or hunters, or intersections of multiple categories, future campaigns may prefer to give volunteers the option to stay within identity groups instead of geographic groups. By steering into the nationalization of politics (Hopkins 2018) rather than anchoring their message in local connections, campaigns could deepen the nationalization of politics to gain electoral advantage.

The 2020 election is likely to serve as a "prototype" (Kreiss 2016) for the use of digital organizing tools in future elections. For Democrats, their digital organizing success in 2020 could be a blueprint for how to efficiently mobilize voters in the future, similar to how Democrats felt after 2008 when the party invested immensely into technology (Kreiss 2016). Democrats have a distinct advantage in this area, not only with more experience utilizing these tactics but also a direct link between Democratic campaign staff and prior work experience in technology-centric fields like data science and analytics (Kreiss 2016). On the Republican side, seeing Biden's success in 2020 without in-person presence could serve as a motivate them to adopt digital organizing tools in the future.

5.2 What Will the Future Hold?

History may be on the verge of repeating itself, as recent candidates turned to non-campaign organizations to do the bulk of their organizing and voter contact. In the 2024 Republican primaries, Ron DeSantis' field operation was mostly controlled by the political action committee (PAC) "Never Back Down." By July 2023, according to press reports, Never Back Down employed 240 canvassers in early voting states with plans to "spend $100 million on the field effort and eventually train 2,600 canvassers" (Anderson 2023). The PAC hired a company called "Blitz Canvassing" to run a $2.8 million door-knocking operation.

While the effort was larger than some of DeSantis' rivals, it also showed the risks of a paid canvasser-based strategy, with quality being the foremost concern. Doorbell cameras captured several examples of inappropriate or ineffective behavior, including a rant from a Never Back Down canvasser who admitted he was "stoned" (Scherer and Dawsey 2023). In echoes of the Dean campaign's woes, Iowa voters did not appreciate the visits from non-locals: "I thought it was off-putting that he was from out of state . . . If you are going to be endorsing or knocking, you need to be from here. I didn't understand why DeSantis of all people could not get other people on the ground" (Scherer and Dawsey 2023). Former Republican congresswoman Barbara Comstock of Virginia described the problem well:

> They're just hiring people who don't even support the candidate. They don't believe in the candidate. Particularly when you're in a competitive primary, you want someone who is local and knows the state and knows the politics of the state,

knows the people, knows who is who. You want people who can speak credibly about a candidate. (Comstock, as quoted in Scherer and Dawsey 2023)

Voters expect candidates to recruit local volunteers in states where retail politics still matters, and using paid out-of-staters indicates weakness.

In 2024, the ground game seems poised to resemble 2012 or 2016 more than 2020. As of May 1, 2024, according to press reports, Biden had opened over 130 offices across several swing states with a heavy investment in states like Wisconsin (44), Michigan (30), and Pennsylvania (24) (Zeleny 2024). Offices are springing up in Nevada and Georgia, two states Democrats are seeking to defend, as well as North Carolina, a state Democrats are trying to flip (Bluestein 2024; Eanes 2024). As of May 2024, we cannot know if the Democratic operation will reach the heights of Obama's or even Clinton's campaigns, but 2020 was clearly not the death knell of storefront campaigning by Democrats.

5.3 Limitations and Future Research

We hope this Element can serve as the basis for future research into the changing context of in-person local organizing as politics nationalizes and digitizes. While it is unlikely that campaigns will ever allow for randomized placement of these offices, future researchers may be able to embed in a campaign during the late spring and early summer months when these decisions are made. A major obstacle to that potential research design, and a limitation of our Element, is that campaign officials are not generally willing to speak to researchers about their strategic decisions. We would have liked to include more insights from different perspectives on this process, from placement decisions to Election Day GOTV operations, but mostly received silence when soliciting interview requests.

The methodological limitations are largely discussed in their respective Sections, but more powerful designs are possible. If individual-level data on voters' addresses and decisions were available, a spatial analysis could speak to the influence of proximity to an office on vote choice and turnout. A large-N survey of campaign staff could shed more light on staff preferences and the benefits they receive from either office-based or distributed organizing (Enos and Hersh 2015). If campaigns were willing to share data on the actual turf assigned to each office, it would be possible to use more targeted precinct-level or census tract data to analyze these effects.

Research into any individual campaign tactic, even those that can be randomized in the field or a lab, is fraught with analytical issues. Campaigns use a package of tactics simultaneously in a condensed time frame, fueled by more a billion dollars, to craft pitches to undecided voters and core partisans alike, and field offices are only one tactic of many.

5.4 All Hands on Deck

Volunteering for a campaign depends upon a voters' available time, skills, and other civic resources, in addition to being asked by a campaign and trained to do so (Rosenstone and Hansen 1993; Verba et al. 1995). This fact should make us cautious about generalizing from the 2020 experience. While it was true that, at least on the Democratic side, there were no offices to go to, people also had far more time on their hands and were stuck inside and bored. The senior Democrat we talked to admitted as much: the success of their digital program was in part a product of the civic resources available to them, not just the effort they put in.

> I also don't know if people would have, had there not been a pandemic where people were just bored at home, I don't think we would have gotten so much out of people. I don't think we would have gotten as much out of people, as many shifts, voter contact, volunteer recruitment from some of our biggest supporters if the rest of their lives were busy because there wouldn't be a pandemic. (senior Democrat, personal communication, September 1, 2022)

This well free time, relative to non-pandemic times, is not likely to be available to campaigns in the future. There will be an expectation that in-person organizing will be provided in the areas where it is most valuable and volunteers ask for it. Those who were brought into political organizing by flexible timing, easy-to-use tools, and online community may still expect that option to be available. The senior Democrat we spoke to seemed confident that in-person and digital could coexist in a campaign:

> There will be a strong emphasis on field offices, but in addition to that a very strong emphasis on the digital. Again, we amassed the biggest mobilization effort in the history of U.S. politics, via many people – that's how they do know how to get involved, and that's how they prefer, and so we have to keep those folks engaged. They are battle-tested, battle-ready. So it's an emphasis on both: reintroducing ourselves to field offices, getting that back up and going – I mean, you look at the Virginia race [in 2021], they had field offices – while also a huge emphasis on the digital and distributed model. (senior Democrat, personal communication, September 1, 2022)

When pressed for details, however, he was unable to say exactly what that will look like in practice. Like so many aspects of presidential campaigns, the airplane may need to be assembled as it rolls down the runway.

> TBD. We still have to see how that will work. . . . There are people who will come into the office and never come back, and we will be able to push them

into the distributed way, and I think vice versa – there will be people who come in through the distributed way, and we will be able to push them into the offices . . . It really does work being able to create that community online and in these virtual spaces. Just imagine how much deeper those connections could be if we could offer them a field office to just meet once together, or to meet – they don't do their work there, but they have team meetings there, they meet every two weeks, just to reinforce those bonds and get them to the next level. (senior Democrat, personal communication, September 1, 2022)

This acknowledgment reaffirms the ultimate reason field offices deserve to remain a part of campaigns: they are a place for people to come together and try to influence politics by having conversations with fellow members of their community. At a time when local news is fading away (Darr et al. 2018) and partisan polarization is on the rise (Mason 2018), it is worth noting and celebrating when both parties rent a storefront, fill it with idealistic young organizers, and send people out to have conversations with their friends and neighbors.

The fact that some outreach can be done digitally is ultimately good for American politics, since it makes participating easier for those who might not otherwise be included in person. Ultimately, however, there is no substitute for the part that keeps people coming back: meeting other activists, surrounded by stickers and stale pizza, picking up the phone or a walk packet and stepping out onto the street to talk to their neighbors.

References

Achen, C., & Bartels, L. (2017). *Democracy for Realists: Why Elections Do Not Produce Responsive Government*. Princeton University Press.

Addonizio, E. M., Green, D. P., & Glaser, J. M. (2007). "Putting the Party Back into Politics: An Experiment Testing whether Election Day Festivals Increase Voter Turnout." *PS: Political Science & Politics*, *40*(4), 721–727.

Alter, C. (August 6, 2020). "Inside the Democrats' Plan to Win Back the Internet." *Time*, https://time.com/5876600/joe-biden-internet-2020-election/

Anderson, Z. (August 1, 2023). "Never Back Down PAC Spent $34 Million for DeSantis with Little to Show for It." *The Herald-Tribune*, www.heraldtribune.com/story/news/politics/2023/07/31/desantis-badly-trails-in-polls-despite-34-million-in-pac-spending/70502996007/

Ansolabehere, S., Luks, S., & Schaffner, B. (2017). *Cooperative Congressional Election Study (CCES) Common Content*. Doi: 10.7910/DVN/II2DB6.

Bailey, M. A., Hopkins, D. J., & Rogers, T. (2016). "Unresponsive and Unpersuaded: The Unintended Consequences of a Voter Persuasion Effort." *Political Behavior*, *38*, 713–746.

Bajak, F., & Burke, G. (November 6, 2020). "Incendiary Texts Traced to Outfit Run by Top Trump Aide." *Associated Press*, https://apnews.com/article/election-2020-joe-biden-donald-trump-pennsylvania-philadelphia-226886a61b7e7ba30af515736e378978

Baldwin-Philippi, J. (2016). "The Cult(ure) of Analytics in 2014." In *Communication and Midterm Elections: Media, Message, and Mobilization* J. A. Hendricks and D. Schill (Eds). (pp. 25–42). Springer.

Barone, M., & Cohen, R. (2006). *The Almanac of American Politics*. National Journal Group.

Berenson, T. (September 20, 2019). "Why the Trump Campaign Says It's Betting on Grassroots Organizing in 2020." *Time*, https://time.com/5672146/donald-trump-2020-campaign-volunteers-obama/

Besta, T., Jaśkiewicz, M., Kosakowska-Berezecka, N., Lawendowski, R., & Zawadzka, A. M. (2018). "What Do I Gain from Joining Crowds? Does Self-Expansion Help to Explain the Relationship between Identity Fusion, Group Efficacy and Collective Action?" *European Journal of Social Psychology*, *48*(2), O152–O167.

Bluestein, G. (April 5, 2024). "Joe Biden's Campaign Is Staffing Up and Opening New Offices in Georgia." *The Atlanta Journal-Constitution*, www.ajc.com/politics/joe-bidens-campaign-is-staffing-up-and-opening-new-offices-in-georgia/QRJZ5U7CKRGT3PCYSQPIT7UI6Q/

Broockman, D., & Kalla, J. (2016). "Durably Reducing Transphobia: A Field Experiment on Door-to-Door Canvassing." *Science*, *352*(6282), 220–224.

Burns, D., & Smith, A. (June 16, 2023). "Inside the $100 Million Door-Knocking Effort to Boost Ron DeSantis." *NBC News*, www.nbcnews.com/politics/2024-election/100-million-door-knocking-effort-boost-ron-desantis-rcna89517

Campbell, J. E. (2008). *The American Campaign: U.S. Presidential Campaigns and the National Vote*. Texas AM University Press.

Chen, L. J., & Reeves, A. (2011). "Turning Out the Base or Appealing to the Periphery? An Analysis of County-Level Candidate Appearances in the 2008 Presidential Campaign." *American Politics Research*, *39*(3), 534–556.

Chetty, R., Jackson, M. O., Kuchler, T., et al. (2022). "Social Capital I: Measurement and Associations with Economic Mobility." *Nature*, *608*(7921), 108–121.

Clinton, H. R. (2017). *What Happened*. Simon and Schuster.

Coppock, A., Hill, S. J., & Vavreck, L. (2020). "The Small Effects of Political Advertising Are Small Regardless of Context, Message, Sender, or Receiver: Evidence from 59 Real-Time Randomized Experiments." *Science Advances*, *6*(36), Eabc4046.

Cox, G. W., & Mccubbins, M. D. (1986). "Electoral Politics as a Redistributive Game." *The Journal of Politics*, *48*(2), 370–389.

Cramer, K. J. (2016). *The Politics of Resentment: Rural Consciousness in Wisconsin and the Rise of Scott Walker*. University of Chicago Press.

Cushman, J. (August 26, 2019). "The Trump Campaign Knows Why Obama Won. Do Democrats?" *The New York Times*, www.nytimes.com/2019/08/26/opinion/republicans-obama-campaign-playbook.html

Dale, A., & Strauss, A. (2009). "Don't forget to vote: Text message reminders as a mobilization tool." *American Journal of Political Science*, *53*(4), 787–804.

Darr, J. P. (October 7, 2016). "Where Clinton Is Setting Up Field Offices – And Where Trump Isn't." *FiveThirtyEight*, https://fivethirtyeight.com/features/trump-clinton-field-offices/

Darr, J. P. (2020). "Polls and Elections: Abandoning the Ground Game? Field Organization in the 2016 Election." *Presidential Studies Quarterly*, *50*(1), 163–175.

Darr, J. P., Hitt, M. P., & Dunaway, J. L. (2018). "Newspaper Closures Polarize Voting Behavior." *Journal of Communication*, *68*(6), 1007–1028.

Darr, J. P., Hitt, M. P., & Dunaway, J. L. (2021). *Home Style Opinion: How Local Newspapers Can Slow Polarization*. Cambridge University Press.

Darr, J. P., & Levendusky, M. S. (2014). "Relying on the Ground Game: The Placement and Effect of Campaign Field Offices." *American Politics Research*, *42*(3), 529–548.

Demissie, A. (October 26, 2012). "A Super-Close Look at Ohio, The State that Could Decide It All." *The Grio*, https://thegrio.com/2012/10/26/a-super-close-look-at-ohio-the-state-that-could-decide-it-all/

Des Moines Register. (August 19, 2019). "Iowa Caucus First Impressions: Michael Bennet Pounds Some Truth into the Campaign." *Des Moines Register*, Editorial, www.desmoinesregister.com/story/opinion/editorials/cau cus/2019/08/19/michael-bennet-pounds-some-truth-into-caucus-campaign/ 2013962001/

Eanes, Z. (March 28, 2024). "Biden Campaign Opening 10 Field Offices in North Carolina." *Axios*, www.axios.com/local/raleigh/2024/03/28/biden-campaign-opening-10-field-offices-in-north-carolina

Eldersveld, S. J., & Walton, H. (1982). *Political Parties in American Society.* Springer.

Emanuel, N., & Harrington, E. (2023). "Working Remotely? Selection, Treatment, and the Market for Remote Work." *Selection, Treatment, and the Market for Remote Work (June 2023). FRB of New York Staff Report* (1061).

Emanuel, N., Harrington, E., & Pallais, E. (2023). "The Power of Proximity to Coworkers: Training for Tomorrow or Productivity Today?" *Working Paper*, https://scholar.harvard.edu/sites/scholar.harvard.edu/files/pallais/files/ power_of_proximity_01.pdf.

Enos, R. D., & Hersh, E. D. (2015). "Party Activists as Campaign Advertisers: The Ground Campaign as a Principal-Agent Problem." *American Political Science Review*, *109*(2), 252–278.

Fowler, E. F., & Ridout, T. N. (2013). "Negative, Angry, and Ubiquitous: Political Advertising in 2012." *The Forum* (Vol. 10, No. 4, pp. 51–61).

Frey, W. (November 13, 2020). "Biden's Victory Came from the Suburbs." *Brookings*, www.brookings.edu/articles/bidens-victory-came-from-the-suburbs/

Ganz, M. L. (2009). "Organizing Obama: Campaign, Organization, Movement." *In the Proceedings of the American Sociological Association Annual Meeting San Francisco, CA, August 8–11, 2009.*

Gerber, A. S., & Green, D. P. (2000). "The Effects of Canvassing, Telephone Calls, and Direct Mail on Voter Turnout: A Field Experiment." *American Political Science Review*, *94*(3), 653–663.

Gerber, A. S., Green, D. P., & Larimer, C. W. (2008). "Social Pressure and Voter Turnout: Evidence from A Large-Scale Field Experiment." *American Political Science Review*, *102*(1), 33–48.

Green, D. P., & Gerber, A. S. (2019). *Get Out the Vote: How to Increase Voter Turnout*. Brookings Institution Press.

Habeck, A. (November 6, 2020). "Comparing How the City and Every Milwaukee County Suburb Voted in 2016 and 2020." *Milwaukee Magazine*, www.milwaukeemag.com/comparing-how-the-city-and-every-milwaukee-county-suburb-voted-in-2016-and-2020/

Heersink, B., Peterson, B. D., & Peterson, J. C. (2021). "Mobilization and Countermobilization: The Effect of Candidate Visits on Campaign Donations in the 2016 Presidential Election." *The Journal of Politics*, *83*(4), 1878–1883.

Hersh, E. D. (2015). *Hacking the Electorate: How Campaigns Perceive Voters*. Cambridge University Press.

Hess, C. (February 8, 2020). "GOP Opens First Milwaukee Field Office." *Urban Milwaukee*, https://urbanmilwaukee.com/2020/02/08/gop-opens-first-milwaukee-field-office/

Hill, S. J., Lo, J., Vavreck, L., & Zaller, J. (2013). "How Quickly We Forget: The Duration of Persuasion Effects from Mass Communication." *Political Communication*, *30*(4), 521–547.

Hopkins, D. J. (2018). *The Increasingly United States: How and Why American Political Behavior Nationalized*. University of Chicago Press.

Issenberg, S. (2012). *The Victory Lab: The Secret Science of Winning Campaigns*. Crown.

Kalla, J. L., & Broockman, D. E. (2020). "Reducing Exclusionary Attitudes through Interpersonal Conversation: Evidence from Three Field Experiments." *American Political Science Review*, *114*(2), 410–425.

King, M., & Bender, M. C. (March 13, 2024). "R.N.C. Shutting Down Community Centers Aimed at Minority Outreach." *New York Times*, www.nytimes.com/2024/03/13/us/politics/republican-community-centers-closed.html

Kreiss, D. (2016). *Prototype Politics: Technology-Intensive Campaigning and the Data of Democracy*. Oxford University Press.

Leary, M. R., & Baumeister, R. (1995). "The Need to Belong." *Psychological Bulletin*, *117*(3), 497–529.

Levendusky, M. S., Pope, J. C., & Jackman, S. D. (2008). "Measuring District-Level Partisanship with Implications for the Analysis of US Elections." *The Journal of Politics*, *70*(3), 736–753.

Malhotra, N., Michelson, M. R., Rogers, T., & Valenzuela, A. A. (2011). "Text Messages as Mobilization Tools: The Conditional Effect of Habitual Voting and Election Salience." *American Politics Research*, *39*(4), 664–681.

Masket, S. (2009). Did Obama's Ground Game Matter? The Influence of Local Field Offices during the 2008 Presidential Election. *Public Opinion Quarterly, 73*(5), 1023–1039.

Masket, S. (2020). *Learning from Loss: The Democrats, 2016–2020.* Cambridge University Press.

Masket, S., Sides, J., & Vavreck, L. (2016). "The Ground Game in the 2012 Presidential Election." *Political Communication, 33*(2), 169–187.

Mason, L. (2018). Uncivil Agreement: *How Politics Became Our Identity.* Chicago: University of Chicago Press.

McClelland, D. C. (1985). "How Motives, Skills, and Values Determine What People Do." *American Psychologist, 40*(7), 812.

McKenna, E., & Han, H. (2014). *Groundbreakers: How Obama's 2.2 Million Volunteers Transformed Campaigning in America.* Oxford University Press.

McRoberts, F. (January 15, 2004). "Perfect Storm Sweeps into Iowa for Dean." *The Chicago Tribune,* www.chicagotribune.com/news/ct-xpm-2004-01-15-0401150391-story.html

Mekelburg, M. (August 23, 2022). "Beto O'Rourke Campaign Seeks to Knock On 5 Million Doors before November Election." *Austin American-Statesman,* www.statesman.com/story/news/politics/state/2022/08/23/beto-orourke-texas-governor-campaign-plans-knock-5-milllion-doors/65414413007/

Miller, M. (2010). "Alinsky for the Left: The Politics of Community Organizing." *Dissent, 57*(1), 43–49.

Munis, B. K., & Burke, R. (2023). "Talk Local to Me: Assessing the Heterogenous Effects of Localistic Appeals." *American Politics Research,* 51(5), 655–669.

Nickerson, D. W. (2006). "Volunteer Phone Calls Can Increase Turnout: Evidence from Eight Field Experiments." *American Politics Research, 34*(3), 271–292.

Nickerson, D. W. (2007). "Quality Is Job One: Professional and Volunteer Voter Mobilization Calls." *American Journal of Political Science, 51*(2), 269–282.

Nickerson, D. W., & Rogers, T. (2010). "Do You Have a Voting Plan? Implementation Intentions, Voter Turnout, and Organic Plan Making." *Psychological Science, 21*(2), 194–199.

Nielsen, R. K. (2012). *Ground Wars: Personalized Communication in Political Campaigns.* Princeton University Press.

Ohme, J., Marquart, F., & Kristensen, L. M. (2020). "School Lessons, Social Media and Political Events in a Get-Out-The-Vote Campaign: Successful Drivers of Political Engagement among Youth?" *Journal of Youth Studies, 23*(7), 886–908.

Panagopoulos, C. (2016). "All about That Base: Changing Campaign Strategies in U.S. Presidential Elections." *Party Politics, 22*(2), 179–190.

Panagopoulos, C. (2020). *Bases Loaded: How U.S. Presidential Campaigns Are Changing and Why It Matters*. Oxford University Press.

Putnam, R. D. (2000). *Bowling Alone: The Collapse and Revival of American Community*. Simon and Schuster.

Ranney, A. (1956). *Democracy and the American Party System*. Harcourt, Brace.

Reese, E., & Whitehouse, H. (2021). "The Development of Identity Fusion." *Perspectives on Psychological Science, 16*(6), 1398–1411.

Rosenstone, S. J., & Hansen, J. M. (1993). *Mobilization, Participation, and Democracy in America*. New York: Macmillan Publishing Company.

Ruiz, R. (February 13, 2020a). "The Bloomberg Campaign Is a Waterfall of Cash." *The New York Times*, www.nytimes.com/2020/02/13/us/politics/bloomberg-campaign-cash.html

Ruiz, R. (March 10, 2020b). "Bloomberg's Job Security Promises Are Falling Through, Campaign Workers Say." *The New York Times*, www.nytimes.com/2020/03/10/us/politics/bloomberg-campaign-staff.html

Scala, D. J., & Johnson, K. M. (2017). "Political Polarization along the Rural-Urban Continuum? The Geography of the Presidential Vote, 2000–2016." *The ANNALS of the American Academy of Political and Social Science, 672*(1), 162–184.

Schaffner, B., Ansolabehere, S., & Luks, S. (2021). "Cooperative Election Study Common Content, 2020." *Harvard Dataverse*.

Schaper, D. (June 13, 2007). "'Camp Obama' Trains Campaign Volunteers." *NPR*, www.npr.org/templates/story/story.php?storyId=11012254

Schein, A., Vafa, K., Sridhar, D., Veitch, V., Quinn, J., Moffet, J., & Green, D. P. (2021). "Assessing the Effects of Friend-to-Friend Texting on Turnout in the 2018 US Midterm Elections." Proceedings of the Web Conference 2021, 2025–2036.

Scherer, M., Dawsey, J. (July 14, 2023). "Door-Knocker Complaints Show Risks of DeSantis Super PAC Strategy." *The Washington Post*, www.washingtonpost.com/politics/2023/07/14/desantis-never-back-down-canvassers/

Schultz, B. (2009). "Obama's Political Philosophy: Pragmatism, Politics, and the University of Chicago." *Philosophy of the Social Sciences, 39*(2), 127–173.

Sesin, C. (October 2, 2020). "What's behind Trump's Gain in Cuban American Support?" *NBC News*, www.nbcnews.com/news/latino/what-s-behind-trump-s-gain-cuban-american-support-n1241601

Shaw, D. R. (2006). *The Race to 270: The Electoral College and the Campaign Strategies of 2000 and 2004*. University Of Chicago Press.

Sides, J., Tesler, M., & Vavreck, L. (2018). *Identity Crisis: The 2016 Presidential Campaign and the Battle for the Meaning of America*. Princeton University Press.

Sinclair, B., McConnell, M., & Michelson, M. R. (2013). "Local Canvassing: The Efficacy of Grassroots Voter Mobilization." *Political Communication*, *30*(1), 42–57.

Singer, N. (November 5, 2022). "Fed Up with Political Text Messages? Read On." *The New York Times*, www.nytimes.com/2022/11/05/technology/polit ical-text-messages-pelosi-trump.html

Skocpol, T., Ganz, M., & Munson, Z. (2000). "A Nation of Organizers: The Institutional Origins of Civic Voluntarism in the United States." *American Political Science Review*, *94*(3), 527–546.

Stacker. (July 25, 2022). "Most Rural Counties in Wisconsin." *Stacker*, https:// stacker.com/wisconsin/most-rural-counties-wisconsin.

Stein, A. (1986). "Between Organization and Movement: Acorn and the Alinsky Model of Community Organizing." *Berkeley Journal of Sociology*, *31*, 93–115.

Stromer-Galley, J. (2014). *Presidential Campaigning in the Internet Age*. Oxford University Press.

Swann, W. B., Jetten, J., Gómez, Á., Whitehouse, H., & Bastian, B. (2012). "When Group Membership Gets Personal: A Theory of Identity Fusion." *Psychological Review*, *119*(3), 441.

Swasey, B., & Jin, C. H. (December 2, 2020). "Narrow Wins in These Key States Powered Biden to the Presidency." *NPR*, www.npr.org/2020/12/02/ 940689086/narrow-wins-in-these-key-states-powered-biden-to-the-presidency

Tausanovitch, C., & Warshaw, C. (2014). "Representation in Municipal Government." *American Political Science Review*, *108*(3), 605–641.

Thompson, A. (August 4, 2020). "Trump's Campaign Knocks on a Million Doors a Week: Biden's Knocks on Zero." *Politico*, www.politico.com/news/ 2020/08/04/trump-joe-biden-campaign-door-knockers-391454

Thomson-DeVeaux, A. (March 2, 2020). "Bloomberg Bet Big on California: It Might Not Pay Off." *FiveThirtyEight*, https://fivethirtyeight.com/features/ bloomberg-bet-big-on-california-it-might-not-pay-off/

Tocqueville, A. (2003). *Democracy in America: And Two Essays on America*. Penguin.

Van Oot, T. (October 7, 2022). "The Door Wars Are Back: Minnesota Candidates Hit 1 Million Voter Homes in Battle for Capitol." *Axios Twin Cities*, www.axios.com/local/twin-cities/2022/10/07/minnesota-legislature-races-campaign-doorknocking

Verba, S., Schlozman, K. L., & Brady, H. E. (1995). *Voice and Equality: Civic Voluntarism in American Politics*. Harvard University Press.

Wamsley, L. (December 24, 2019). "Bloomberg Campaign Vendor Used Prison Labor to Make Presidential Campaign Calls." *NPR*, www.npr.org/2019/12/24/791194618/bloomberg-campaign-vendor-used-prison-labor-to-make-presidential-campaign-calls.

Weinschenk, A. C. (2015). "Polls and Elections: Campaign Field Offices and Voter Mobilization in 2012." *Presidential Studies Quarterly, 45*(3), 573–580.

Whitehouse, H., & Lanman, J. A. (2014). "The Ties that Bind Us: Ritual, Fusion, and Identification." *Current Anthropology, 55*(6), 674–695.

Williamson, E. (January 23, 2012). "Two Ways to Play the 'Alinsky' Card." *The Wall Street Journal*, www.wsj.com/articles/SB10001424052970204624204577177272926154002.

Yaden, D. B., Haidt, J., Hood Jr., R. W., Vago, D. R., & Newberg, A. B. (2017). "The Varieties of Self-Transcendent Experience." *Review of General Psychology, 21*(2), 143–160.

Yan, A. N., & Bernhard, R. (2024). "The Silenced Text: Field Experiments on Gendered Experiences of Political Participation." *American Political Science Review, 118*(1), 481–487.

Yudkin, D. A., Gantman, A. P., Hofmann, W., & Quoidbach, J. (2021). "Binding Moral Values Gain Importance in the Presence of Close Others." *Nature Communications, 12*(1), 2718.

Yudkin, D. A., Prosser, A. M., Heller, S. M., et al. (2022). "Prosocial Correlates of Transformative Experiences at Secular Multi-Day Mass Gatherings." *Nature Communications, 13*(1), 2600.

Zaller, J. (1992). *The Nature and Origins of Mass Opinion*. Cambridge University Press.

Zeleny, J. (April 30, 2024). "Biden's Growing Tally of Campaign Offices Marks a Rare Bright Spot for the President." *CNN*, www.cnn.com/2024/04/30/politics/biden-campaign-offices-election/index.html

Acknowledgements

We are grateful to the many people who helped this project become a reality. Joshua would like to thank his family, first and foremost, for their constant support; Matthew Levendusky for nurturing this idea and trusting a graduate student with the data collection; Hahrie Han for generous discussions and insight about this topic; and the Gasparoni family of Coralville, Iowa for their hospitality during his 2019 research trip. Sean would like to thank Joshua Darr for his willingness to partner with a graduate student on this project; his colleague from New Hampshire, Peter O'Neill, for agreeing to speak with the authors; the other interviewees who shared their perspectives; and his family for their unwavering support and nonstop encouragement throughout the process. The editors and writers at FiveThirtyEight (including Micah Cohen, Sarah Frostenson, and Nathaniel Rakich), as well as Seth Masket at Mischiefs of Faction, provided excellent feedback and invaluable platforms for this work as it was in progress. We thank many conference attendees over the past decade for their comments, our editor Emily Beaulieu Bacchus for her stewardship throughout the process, and the anonymous reviewers for improving the manuscript. Any errors or omissions are our own.

Cambridge Elements ☰

Campaigns and Elections

R. Michael Alvarez

California Institute of Technology

R. Michael Alvarez is Professor of Political and Computational Social Science at Caltech. His current research focuses on election administration and technology, campaigns and elections, and computational modeling.

Emily Beaulieu Bacchus

University of Kentucky

Emily Beaulieu Bacchus is Associate Professor of Political Science and Director of International Studies at the University of Kentucky. She is an expert in political institutions and contentious politics—focusing much of her work on perceptions of election fraud and electoral protests. Electoral Protest and Democracy in the Developing World was published with Cambridge University Press in 2014.

Charles Stewart III

Massachusetts Institute of Technology

Charles Stewart III is the Kenan Sahin Distinguished Professor of Political Science at MIT. His research and teaching focus on American politics, election administration, and legislative politics.

About the Series

Broadly focused, covering electoral campaigns & strategies, voting behavior, and electoral institutions, this Elements series offers the opportunity to publish work from new and emerging fields, especially those at the interface of technology, elections, and global electoral trends.

Cambridge Elements ☰

Campaigns and Elections

Printed in the United States
by Baker & Taylor Publisher Services